Knowledge to navigate a changing world

THE STATE OF DISCIPLESHIP

Research conducted among Christian adults, church leaders, exemplar discipleship ministries and Christian educators

Research commissioned by:
The Navigators, Colorado Springs, Colorado

Research conducted by:
Barna Group, Ventura, California

The State of Discipleship © 2015 by The Navigators. All rights reserved.

ISBN 978-0-9965843-2-6

All information contained in this document is copyrighted by The Navigators and shall remain the property of The Navigators. U.S. and international copyright laws protect the contents of this document in their entirety. Any reproduction, modification, distribution, transmission, paublication, translation, display, hosting or sale of all or any portion of the contents of this document is strictly prohibited without written permission of an authorized representative of The Navigators.

The information contained in this report is true and accurate to the best knowledge of the researchers and the copyright holder. It is provided without warranty of any kind: express, implied or otherwise. In no event shall The Navigators, NavPress, Barna Group or their employees be liable for any special, incidental, indirect or consequential damages of any kind, or any damages whatsoever resulting from the use of this information, whether or not users have been advised of the possibility of damage, or on any theory of liability, arising out of or in connection with the use of this information.

Unless otherwise indicated, Scripture quotations are from the *New Living Translation* copyright ©1996, 2004, 2007, 2013 by Tyndale House Foundation. Used by permission of Tyndale House Publishers Inc., Carol Stream, Illinois 60188. All rights reserved.

Scripture quotations labeled *Message* (*MSG*) are from *The Message* by Eugene H. Peterson, copyright © 1993, 1993, 1995, 2000, 2001, 2002. Used by permission of NavPress Publishing Group. All rights reserved.

CONTENTS

Foreword by Doug Nuenke 5
Introduction 7
Executive Summary 9
"Discipleship in Future Tense" by David Kinnaman 13
Data Analysis 17

    1. **Defining Discipleship** 19
        Scripture-Shaped Discipleship 30
    2. **Spiritual Health** 35
        Q&A with Mike Jordahl 41
    3. **Discipleship Models** 45
        Q&A with Lindy Black 54
    4. **Obstacles** 57
        "The Spiritual Landscape Has Changed"
        by Fran Sciacca 61
    5. **Commitment** 65
    6. **Assessment** 69
        "Four Reflections on the State of Discipleship"
        by Preston Sprinkle 71
    7. **Resources** 75
    8. **Millennials** 83
        Barna Group on Millennials 87

Implications & Recommendations 89

Appendices 93

    A. Data Tables 94
    B. Educators 137
    C. Exemplars 140
    D. Methodologies 143

About Barna 144

FOREWORD

Since 1933, The Navigators have had discipleship and disciplemaking at our core. In those early years, helping people know, love and follow Christ was the burden Dawson Trotman carried with him as he initiated conversations with young Navy men and encouraged them to do the same. Before long, multiple spiritual generations of "Navigators" were nurturing their own walk with God even as they reproduced the faith in the people around them—where they lived, worked and played.

The Navigators are by no means the only, let alone the first, organized movement of discipleship and disciplemaking. This was, of course, the Great Commission Jesus offered His followers at the end of His earthly ministry:

> Go out and train everyone you meet, far and near, in this way of life, marking them by baptism in the threefold name: Father, Son, and Holy Spirit. Then instruct them in the practice of all I have commanded you. I'll be with you as you do this, day after day after day, right up to the end of the age. (Matthew 28:19-20, *MSG*)

The Great Commission is an audacious undertaking, all the more so given the fast and sweeping changes taking place in the broader culture. As we continue to bring the unchanging message of the Gospel to our friends and neighbors, effective approaches to discipleship become more important, especially in a world that is increasingly polarized around spiritual issues.

That's why The Navigators commissioned the research presented in this monograph. We wanted to hear from laypeople and leaders, professors and practitioners, across the spectrum of American Christianity, about what is getting in the way of following Jesus in our world, and what is proving effective in knowing Christ and making Him known. As an organization we'll be wrestling with the findings in this report as we continue our participation in the Great Commission. We hope that our friends and collaborators from other Christian missions and movements will similarly find this research to be helpful as they tend to the people God has brought under their care. Together in spirit, we will continue the good work of the Great Commission, and we look forward to seeing the fruit of our labors as God works in and through us.

Doug Nuenke
U.S. President
The Navigators

INTRODUCTION

What is the current state of discipleship in the U.S.? How is it defined? What are the hallmarks of transformative discipleship, and how do we measure its outcomes? What resources and models are necessary for effective discipleship in the 21st century? And how do The Navigators' discipleship methods and resources align with the needs of the Church?

To answer these questions, The Navigators and NavPress commissioned Barna Group to undertake a comprehensive, multi-phase research study.

The first phase was a series of in-depth interviews of 36 educators from Protestant and Catholic seminaries and Bible colleges, conducted online in December 2014 and January 2015.

The second phase included in-depth interviews with leaders of 30 churches and seven parachurch ministries that exemplify excellence in discipleship. These "exemplars" completed an open-ended, online survey in February 2015. Participants were identified by Navigators staff or nominated by Protestant pastors from Barna's Pastor Panel.

Next, a total of 2,003 self-identified Christians, including 1,237 practicing Christians, participated in a survey conducted online and by telephone in March and April 2015. Practicing Christians are self-identified Christians who attended a Christian church service at least once during the past month and say their religious faith is very important in their life today.

Barna also wanted to discover how closely the perspectives of those connected with The Navigators compare to other U.S. Christians. To that end, Navigators invited people formerly discipled through the organization to complete the Christian population survey described above. Where relevant, the data on Navigators alumni are presented in this report alongside the findings among other Christian adults for ease of comparison.

The final phase of research consisted of 833 online and telephone interviews conducted in April and May 2015 with Protestant senior pastors and congregational leaders who specialize in discipleship and spiritual growth. A total of 615 interviews were conducted with senior pastors and 218 with discipleship leaders. (In the following report, senior pastors and discipleship leaders are, more often than not, analyzed as one larger group called "church leaders." Where significant differences between the two groups exist, these are highlighted.)

EXECUTIVE SUMMARY

A critical component of this study is to *define* "discipleship." The concept is familiar to many, but a widely accepted definition remains elusive. Although it may seem a mere technicality, accurate and relevant terminology and a clear definition are important first steps toward ensuring a church or ministry can effectively grow disciples.

The preferred terms of various groups are helpful, though not definitive, in revealing their priorities and preconceptions. Christian adults and church leaders alike most commonly prefer "becoming more Christ-like" to describe the process of spiritual growth. Approximately half of both populations select this terminology.

With the term "discipleship" there is a gap between leader and lay language: Only 17 percent of Christian adults prefer "discipleship" compared with 46 percent of church leaders. Importantly, however, the term is considered "relevant" by 65 percent of Christians who do not choose "discipleship" as their top preference.

Accordingly, the reported *goals* of discipleship mirror "becoming more Christ-like." Church leaders prioritize life transformation ("being transformed to become more like Jesus," 89%), while Christian adults are somewhat more outcomes-focused ("learning to live a more consistent Christian life," 60%, and "learning to trust in God more," 59%). Leaders from exemplar churches validate these goals; many report a shift away from an emphasis purely on knowledge toward life transformation.

Making disciples, or "winning new believers to become followers of Jesus Christ," is the least-commonly chosen goal of discipleship. Nevertheless, nearly half of the surveyed populations consider this important: 46 percent of Christian adults and 59 percent of church leaders.

How well do churches "do" discipleship? Christian adults have positive impressions: 52 percent of those who have attended church in the past six months say their church "definitely does a good job helping people grow spiritually" and another 40 percent say it "probably" does so. Church leaders, however, are unconvinced: *Only 1 percent* say "today's churches

> **CHRISTIAN ADULTS AND CHURCH LEADERS ALIKE MOST COMMONLY PREFER "BECOMING MORE CHRIST-LIKE" TO DESCRIBE THE PROCESS OF SPIRITUAL GROWTH.**

are doing very well at discipling new and young believers." Sixty percent feel churches are discipling "not too well." Looking at their own church, 8 percent say they are doing "very well" and 56 percent "somewhat well" at discipling new and young believers.

Self-reported participation in discipleship activities (Sunday school, spiritual mentoring, group Bible study or Christian book study) is weak—as low as 20 percent—indicating that church leaders' assessment of discipleship effectiveness may be more accurate than their parishioners'. Against the overall trend of low involvement, discipleship leaders estimate approximately half of their members are in some sort of discipleship group or relationship. This suggests that churches with a dedicated discipleship leader are able to engage more of the flock in spiritual growth practices, activities or disciplines.

Navigators alumni responses reveal a healthy faith and deep commitment to Navigators' core tenets of discipleship. In fact, they are more likely to resemble church leaders in their answers than the general population.

BARRIERS TO DISCIPLESHIP

Such low participation invites an obvious question: *Are there significant barriers to participation in discipleship activities?*

All the groups Barna interviewed—Christian adults, church leaders, exemplars and educators—agree on the two most significant barriers to spiritual growth: the general "busyness" of life and a lack of commitment to discipleship. However, church leaders and Christian adults disagree significantly on the *magnitude* of these barriers. For example, 85 percent of church leaders say busyness is a major obstacle to discipleship, while only 23 percent of practicing Christians say the same. In fact, *none* of the barriers presented as options to Christian adults resonate as a major obstacle with more than one-quarter of respondents.

In addition to low rates of participation in discipleship activities, further evidence of general spiritual apathy comes from the one in

ALL GROUPS AGREE ON THE TWO MOST SIGNIFICANT BARRIERS TO SPIRITUAL GROWTH: THE GENERAL "BUSYNESS" OF LIFE AND A LACK OF COMMITMENT TO DISCIPLESHIP.

10 Christians who say their spiritual growth is "not too" or "not at all" important: Two-thirds of *these* say they are comfortable with where they are spiritually. Among a significant number of Christians today, there is simply no drive to prioritize spiritual growth.

Additionally, an isolationist approach to spiritual growth is common among U.S. Christians. Among those who consider spiritual growth very or somewhat important (90%), nearly two in five prefer to pursue growth on their own (37%). One-quarter prefers a small group (25%); 16 percent prefer the one-on-one approach; and one in five likes a mix of these methods (21%). Notably, Millennials are more likely to prefer one-on-one discipleship (21% vs. 14% of Gen-Xers and 16% of Boomers and Elders).

Church leaders prefer a small group format (52%) nearly two-to-one over mentoring (29%); mainline pastors prefer small groups even more than the average. Exemplar church leaders, however, widely consider a one-on-one component essential to fruitful discipleship.

Among the 90 percent of Christians who believe spiritual growth is important, one-quarter are being discipled by someone (one-on-one, 23%) and one in five is discipling another person (19%). The primary barrier cited by those who are engaged in neither relationship is a lack of priority. Twenty-nine percent of those not being discipled say they simply "have not thought about it," while 25 percent do not believe they need to be discipled by someone else.

AN ISOLATIONIST APPROACH TO SPIRITUAL GROWTH IS COMMON AMONG U.S. CHRISTIANS.

INDICATORS OF EFFECTIVE DISCIPLESHIP

A healthy culture of discipleship, according to exemplar leaders, appears to be created by 1) senior leadership and 2) a clear plan. Three-quarters of exemplar respondents say senior leadership vision or endorsement is critical to their efforts, along with a clearly articulated approach to discipleship. Among all church leaders, 26 percent say discipleship is their number-one priority, and another 61 percent list it among their top three priorities.

When asked how they want to improve in their discipleship programs, a plurality of church leaders says they would "develop a more clearly

A HEALTHY CULTURE OF DISCIPLESHIP, ACCORDING TO EXEMPLAR LEADERS, APPEARS TO BE CREATED BY 1) SENIOR LEADERSHIP AND 2) A CLEAR PLAN.

articulated plan or approach to discipleship" (27%). Additionally, churches need to develop assessment criteria to track the effectiveness of their discipleship efforts. Less than 1 percent of leaders report using a survey or other evaluation instrument to assess the results of their programs.

With regard to resources, there is a general desire for materials. Fifty-nine percent of church leaders believe it is "very valuable" for Christians to be involved in a systematic curriculum or program of discipleship. However, two out of three believe there are enough—or more than enough—discipleship materials currently available.

IN SUM

Churches are in need of new models for discipleship. Current programs capture only a minority of Christians, and most believers do not prioritize an investment in their spiritual growth. At the same time, church leaders desire a clear plan and lack systems to evaluate spiritual health. Millennials, as we will see—though time-starved and distracted—crave relationships, especially one-on-one. Each of these needs aligns with Navigators' approach to discipleship, suggesting opportunities to provide much-needed influence and guidance.

DISCIPLESHIP IN FUTURE TENSE

David Kinnaman

Research usually examines a subject matter in the present tense.

A good example is this project: the *state* of discipleship. In fact, we completed this study in partnership with the Navigators in order to understand the current reality of discipleship—how it's defined, how it works, what keeps people from growing as disciples. Beyond the anecdotes, these pages contain many insights into what is actually happening with the Church's discipleship efforts.

In addition to describing the present reality, however, good research can help us to think in *future tense*. What might we change to create a different and better set of spiritual outcomes? If we are concerned about the current reality of discipleship—and the findings suggest we should be—what changes can we make today that will shape the future of making and forming disciples?

We hope this research—expressed in infographics, charts, tables and narrative analysis—helps you to envision your future contribution to Jesus' Great Commission.

THE URGENCY OF FUTURE THINKING

Thinking about our future together as Christ-followers is an urgent matter. Here are three reasons this is so important:

- **The Screen Age.** The digital era is creating a new cultural context for and intensifying the pressures facing the Church. The "Screen Age" has exponentially increased access to information about life and how to live it that, paradoxically, both augments and competes with biblical wisdom. The Internet and social technology have also created a new outlet for questions about the nature of authority, and especially about the truth claims of the Bible. We believe that technology can be both friend and foe when it comes to discipleship, but either way there's little doubt it's changing the rules of spiritual formation.

- **The Distracted Era.** One of the reasons technology is changing our spiritual context is that it contributes to unprecedented levels of distraction. But it's not just our screens that suck us in. People are busier than ever with things like kids' sports, increased workloads, and recreation and leisure activities. Humans simply are over-choiced with ways to spend their time. In the spiritual arena, people who consider themselves "regular churchgoers" attend church fewer weekends per year and are often less involved in their faith community's rhythm of communal life.

- **The Shift to Self.** A third macro-trend affecting the discipleship landscape is the rise of the individual as the center of everything. Original sin created the self-absorption problem in the first place, but we live in a comparatively narcissistic era. Whether because of consumerism's tentacles, or the instant gratification of digital tools, or some combination of other factors, more people are "all about me."

  - 84% of adults in the U.S., and 66% of practicing Christians, agree that "the highest goal for life is to enjoy it as much as possible."
  - 91% of adults, and 76% of practicing Christians, believe that "the best way to find yourself is to look inside yourself."
  - 97% of adults, and 91% of practicing Christians, agree that "you have to be true to yourself."

This mindset especially affects the work of discipleship. If we peel back the layers, many Christians are using the Way of Jesus as a means of pursuing the Way of Self. Our discipleship efforts must prophetically respond to the "iSpirit" of the age; people must not only convert to become a disciple of Jesus, but also de-convert from the religion of Self.

OPPORTUNITIES FOR DISCIPLESHIP

To address these challenges, the research identifies many opportunities for the Christian community invested in making disciples. For example, the non-practicing Christian segment is an enormous group of people not currently involved in church, but who want to grow spiritually. They indicate that finding someone to help and knowing what next steps to take are significant barriers to the spiritual growth they desire.

Another opportunity: People identify family members and people at church as having had the most significant spiritual impact on them. So empowering disciples to disciple others (family members, someone at church, friends) is an important way churches and discipleship ministries can multiply their impact.

One of the biggest opportunities is also, perhaps, the largest challenge: getting people past their apathy. Apathy is not merely a lack of passion, but a reluctance to dive fully into what God has in store.

How do we help people prioritize discipleship? How can we promote one-on-one discipleship and mentoring relationships? In what ways can we get people to take responsibility for one another and not just their own personal discipleship? And how can we become the generative disciple-makers Jesus calls us to be?

With a firm grip on reality today, we can begin to think in future tense.

PEOPLE MUST NOT ONLY CONVERT TO BECOME A DISCIPLE OF JESUS, BUT ALSO DE-CONVERT FROM THE RELIGION OF SELF.

David Kinnaman is president and owner of Barna Group. He is the author of the bestselling books *You Lost Me* and *unChristian*. Since joining Barna in 1995, David has overseen studies that have polled the opinions and perspectives of more than 750,000 individuals. He has done research for the American Bible Society, Compassion, Dreamworks Animation, Habitat for Humanity, HarperCollins, Navigators, NBC-Universal, Paramount Pictures, the Salvation Army, Sony, Prison Fellowship, World Vision, and many other world-changing organizations.

DATA ANALYSIS

What Is Discipleship?

"DISCIPLESHIP IS A LIFELONG PROCESS AND JOURNEY ROOTED IN A RELATIONSHIP WITH JESUS."

(TOP-RANKED DESCRIPTION OF DISCIPLESHIP AMONG CHRISTIANS)

HOW DO PEOPLE TALK ABOUT DISCIPLESHIP?

THE FOLLOWING ARE THE TERMS CHRISTIANS MOST PREFER FOR "DISCIPLESHIP"

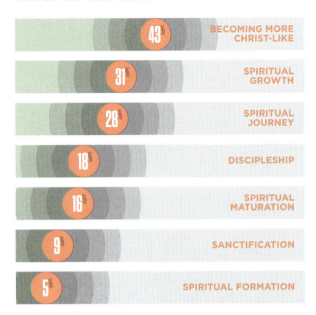

- 43% — BECOMING MORE CHRIST-LIKE
- 31% — SPIRITUAL GROWTH
- 28% — SPIRITUAL JOURNEY
- 18% — DISCIPLESHIP
- 16% — SPIRITUAL MATURATION
- 9% — SANCTIFICATION
- 5% — SPIRITUAL FORMATION

TOP 3 GOALS FOR DISCIPLESHIP

PASTORS AND LAYPEOPLE HAVE VERY DIFFERENT GOALS FOR DISCIPLESHIP

Christians:
1. LEARNING TO LIVE A MORE CONSISTENT CHRISTIAN LIFE — 60%
2. LEARNING TO TRUST IN GOD MORE — 59%
3. KNOWING CHRIST MORE DEEPLY — 58%

Pastors:
1. BEING TRANSFORMED TO BECOME MORE LIKE JESUS — 87%
2. GROWING IN SPIRITUAL MATURITY — 79%
3. KNOWING CHRIST MORE DEEPLY — 78%

1.
DEFINING DISCIPLESHIP

TERMS FOR DISCIPLESHIP

Before we can understand the state of discipleship, we must ask, "What *is* discipleship?" The clearest insight from this study . . . is that it's unclear! Some terms are more preferred than others, and general themes emerge from the data, but Christians and church leaders of all types use a wide range of vocabulary and definitions. Before exploring the practices of discipleship in use today, let's look at the terms, definitions and goals related to this quintessentially Christian idea.

The most common term selected by Christian adults and church leaders alike to describe *the process of spiritual growth* is "becoming more Christ-like." More than half of practicing Christians prefer this term (54%), compared with one-quarter of non-practicing Christians (25%). Half of Protestant church leaders prefer this label (51%). The phrase also echoes the sentiments of leaders in exemplar churches, who most commonly define discipleship as "becoming more like Jesus."

"Discipleship" is a close second among church leaders, with 46 percent preferring this term. Leaders in non-mainline churches (48%) are more likely than those in mainline congregations (36%) to use "discipleship." However, only 17 percent of Christians (23% of practicing Christians) say they use "discipleship." This substantial gap suggests either that church leaders often use a layperson's label to communicate about what they personally think of as "discipleship," or that Christian jargon does not resonate well with the general population—or both.

> "A disciple is one who responds in faith and obedience to the gracious call to follow Jesus Christ. Being a disciple is a lifelong process of dying to self while allowing Jesus to come alive in us."
>
> Christian educator

It is important to note, however, that among the eight in 10 Christians who do *not* prefer "discipleship" (83%), 28 percent still consider the term "very relevant" and another 37 percent consider it "somewhat relevant." Further, four out of 10 practicing Christians who do not prefer "discipleship" (41% vs. 10% of non-practicing Christians) consider the term "very relevant." Thus, although the lay community does not commonly use the term "discipleship," it is still a familiar and understandable term to a substantial majority of Christian adults.

Likewise, among church leaders who do not prefer "discipleship," only 10 percent say their preferred term is *different from* "discipleship." Forty-seven percent say "discipleship" is the same as their term of choice.

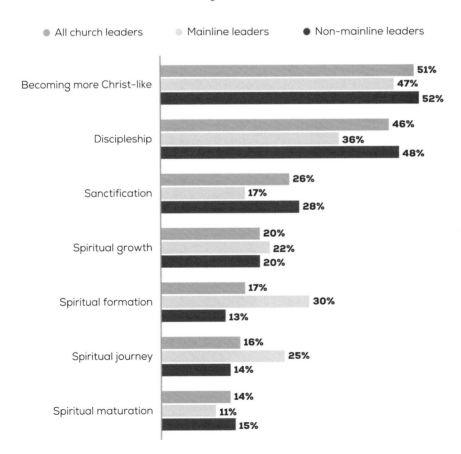

Some exemplar leaders and educators speak about the concept of "spiritual formation" as a newer approach to spiritual growth. Many cite the writings of Richard Foster and Dallas Willard, with educators more narrowly focused on these authors and exemplars citing a broader range of perspectives. However, only 17 percent of church leaders and 5 percent of Christian adults say they use the term "spiritual formation." This concept is more common in mainline churches, in larger faith communities and in Northeastern and Midwestern congregations. Three in 10 mainline church leaders (30%), compared to 13 percent of non-mainline leaders, prefer "spiritual formation."

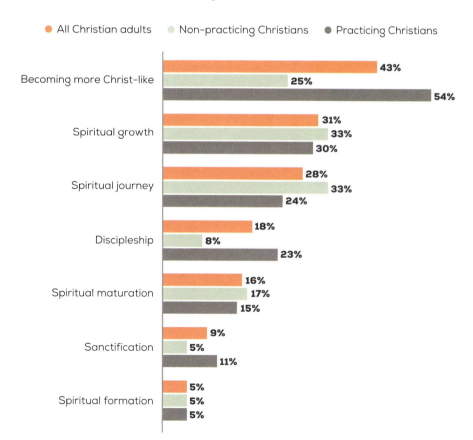

PREFERRED TERMS FOR DISCIPLESHIP
% among Christian adults

● All Christian adults   ● Non-practicing Christians   ● Practicing Christians

Becoming more Christ-like: 43% / 25% / 54%
Spiritual growth: 31% / 33% / 30%
Spiritual journey: 28% / 33% / 24%
Discipleship: 18% / 8% / 23%
Spiritual maturation: 16% / 17% / 15%
Sanctification: 9% / 5% / 11%
Spiritual formation: 5% / 5% / 5%

"Sanctification" is another term used by more leaders than congregants. Nine percent of Christians versus one in four church leaders (26%) prefer "sanctification," and the term is most prevalent in non-mainline (28% vs. 17% mainline) and smaller churches.

Finally, "spiritual journey" is preferred by one in four mainline (25%) and one in seven non-mainline churches (14%), with leaders in the Northeast embracing it most enthusiastically (30% vs. 12% of Southerners and 18% elsewhere). A similar proportion of the general Christian population expresses a preference for this term, with 28 percent selecting "spiritual journey." It is slightly more preferred among non-practicing Christians (33% vs. 24% of practicing Christians).

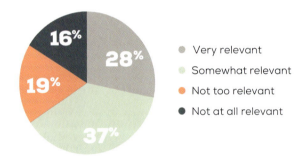

RELEVANCE OF THE TERM "DISCIPLESHIP"
% among Christian adults NOT choosing "discipleship" as preferred term

- Very relevant: 28%
- Somewhat relevant: 37%
- Not too relevant: 19%
- Not at all relevant: 16%

Navigators alumni align closely with church leaders on terminology, with most preferring "becoming more Christ-like" (55%) and "discipleship" (49%), followed closely by "sanctification" (41%). Among those who do not pick "discipleship" as their preference, almost all consider the term "very relevant" (84%).

Compared with the general Christian population, they are less likely to use "spiritual growth" or "spiritual journey."

TERMS USED TO DESCRIBE SPIRITUAL GROWTH

Q: Would you use any of these words to describe the process of spiritual growth?
(Two answers allowed)

	All Church Leaders	Senior Pastors	Discipleship Leaders	All Christians	Practicing Christians	Non-practicing Christians	Navigators Alumni
Becoming more Christ-like	51%	51%	49%	43%	54%	25%	55%
Discipleship	46	45	46	17	23	8	49
Sanctification	26	25	28	9	11	5	41
Spiritual growth	21	20	22	31	30	33	18
Spiritual formation	17	18	16	5	5	5	10
Spiritual journey	16	17	15	28	24	33	2
Spiritual maturation	14	14	14	16	15	17	18
None of these	1	1	1	8	3	18	0
Not sure	0	0	1	1	0	1	0

RELEVANCE OF "DISCIPLESHIP" WHEN DESCRIBING SPIRITUAL GROWTH

Q: Some Christians use the term "discipleship" to describe a process of spiritual growth. How relevant is the term "discipleship" to you, when you think of the process of spiritual growth?

(% among those who did not use "discipleship")

	All Christians	Practicing Christians	Non-practicing Christians	Navigators Alumni
Very relevant	28%	41%	10%	84%
Somewhat relevant	37	40	33	12
Not too relevant	19	12	28	4
Not at all relevant	16	7	28	0
Not sure	1	0	1	0

GOALS OF DISCIPLESHIP

When it comes to defining the goals of discipleship, church leaders, and especially discipleship pastors, do not like to narrow them to a few main objectives. Rather, many select nearly all of the surveyed goals as important outcomes of discipleship. This suggests a sense that there are multiple benefits to discipleship, but perhaps also a general lack of clarity about its purpose.

Goals generally align with the preferred terminology for discipleship (that is, "becoming more Christ-like"). Those most commonly selected by leaders are "being transformed to become more like Jesus" (89%), "growing in spiritual maturity" (83%) and "knowing Christ more deeply" (83%). By contrast, Christian adults overall choose "learning to live a more consistent Christian life" (60%), "learning to trust in God more" (59%) and "knowing Christ more deeply" (58%). These preferences suggest lay Christians focus on outcomes somewhat more than leaders, whose top goals tend to be more transformational.

Exemplars report priorities similar to church leaders. Many say their objectives for discipleship have shifted away from pursuit of "head knowledge" toward life transformation, usually in the context of relationship. For example, one exemplar leader wrote, "The idea/concept of spiritual formation in a postmodern world has greatly expanded the definition to be more organic and relational vs. the transferring of information."

The least-preferred, though still popular, goal of discipleship is conversion. Six in 10 church leaders (59%) and less than half of Christian adults (46%) say "winning new believers to become followers of Jesus Christ" is a primary goal of discipleship. This is consistent, once again, with exemplars, of whom more than half refer to "making disciples" as an important component, but not the *only* goal, of discipleship. Some provide context that their idea of "making disciples" has expanded from only conversion to growing in Christ, because real, healthy disciples should naturally produce more disciples.

The concept of mentoring falls somewhere in the middle: Three-quarters of church leaders (77%) and half of Christian adults (50%) consider "mentoring and being mentored in the area of Christian maturity" an important goal of discipleship.

Notably, 15 percent of non-practicing Christians do not select any goals of discipleship, saying instead that they "don't know or have never thought about it."

Navigators alumni once again resemble church leaders with respect to the goals of discipleship: They have more goals overall, and their primary goal is "being transformed to become more like Jesus" (84%). Other top goals, very closely aligned with the core tenets of the Navigators approach to discipleship, include "mentoring and being mentored in the area of Christian maturity" (74%) and "knowing Christ more deeply" (67%).

> "I used to think of discipleship as gaining head knowledge. I now think of it more as a complete way of life that is best 'caught' instead of 'taught.' I also see discipleship best happening in a culture where one-on-one spiritual conversations are the norm instead of the exception."
>
> Exemplar
> church leader

DEFINITIONS OF DISCIPLESHIP

Developing a single statement that encompasses the definition of discipleship is difficult. Church leaders are relatively split on three definitions, as seen in the table below; the more comprehensive definitions, however, are preferred over simpler forms.

Christian adults, by contrast, express a slight preference for the idea of a "journey rooted in a relationship with Jesus" (ranked an average 2.9 out of 6) and "the process of learning to follow Jesus Christ as Savior and Lord" (ranked 3.0). Yet no definition emerges as a clear winner in a ranking of the six statements.

Those discipled by Navigators appear somewhat like other Christians. Their preferred definition is, "Discipleship is the process of learning to follow Jesus Christ as Savior and Lord, seeking to observe all that Jesus commanded, by the power of the Holy Spirit and to the glory of God the Father" (ranked 2.7).

"What is discipleship? In two words, discipleship could be described as *spiritual parenting*. As 1 Thessalonians 2:3-13 tells us, discipleship involves many of the characteristics you would expect to find in a responsible parent:

- To have single-minded purpose in pleasing God and growing a believer spiritually (vv. 3-6)
- To care for a believer as a mother cares for a child, in word and in deed (vv. 7-8)
- To be a role model to a new believer (vv. 9-10)
- To give individual attention and encouragement as a father (vv. 11-12)
- To help them learn the Word of God (vv. 8,13)

In short, discipleship is not only taught but caught. It is important to teach a disciple the Word and ways of God, but equally important to live out what we teach. The character of the discipler is critical for the formation of the disciple. A disciple will learn both from what you say and what you do."

Christian educator

GOALS OF DISCIPLESHIP

Q: People often have different ways of defining the goal of discipleship. For each of the following please tell me if each term is one you'd use to describe the primary goal or goals of discipleship.

	All Church Leaders	Senior Pastors	Discipleship Leaders	All Christians	Practicing Christians	Non-practicing Christians	Navigators Alumni
Being transformed to become more like Jesus	89%	87%	94%	45%	53%	32%	84%
Growing in spiritual maturity	83	79	94	55	61	46	57
Knowing Christ more deeply	83	78	95	58	65	47	67
Becoming more obedient to God	77	73	88	55	63	42	39
Learning to live a more consistent Christian life	77	72	90	60	66	50	45
Mentoring and being mentored in the area of Christian maturity	77	71	92	50	59	35	74
Learning to trust in God more	75	71	86	59	63	51	39
Deepening one's faith through education and fellowship	72	67	87	56	62	46	35
Winning new believers to become followers of Jesus Christ	59	56	69	46	55	31	33
Don't know / Never thought about it	0	0	0	7	2	15	0

PREFERRED DEFINITIONS OF DISCIPLESHIP:
CHURCH LEADERS

Q: When you think about the idea of discipleship, which one of the following comes closest to how you define it?
(online only; n = 290)

Definition	All Church Leaders
Discipleship is the process where a person purposely joins God to increasingly follow and live like Jesus, through the Scriptures, the Holy Spirit, and the input of others.	26%
Discipleship is the process of learning to follow Jesus Christ as Savior and Lord, seeking to observe all that Jesus commanded, by the power of the Holy Spirit and to the glory of God the Father.	24
Discipleship is the process of transformation that changes us to be increasingly more like Christ through the Word, the Spirit, and circumstance.	20
Discipleship is a lifelong process and journey rooted in a relationship with Jesus.	14
Discipleship is becoming more and more like Jesus and letting Him live His life more and more in me.	8
Discipleship is about connecting with someone who will help you connect with God for the purpose of fulfilling your God-given destiny.	5
Other / none of these	3

RANKING DEFINITIONS OF DISCIPLESHIP:
CHRISTIAN ADULTS

Q: The following are some definitions that some people might use to describe "discipleship." Please rank these phrases in order of which comes closest to how you think about discipleship, where the top (#1) is closest and the bottom (#6) is furthest from how you would describe discipleship.

(mean rank; online survey only; n = 1,300)

	All Christian Adults	Navigators Alumni
Discipleship is a lifelong process and journey rooted in a relationship with Jesus.	2.9	3.9
Discipleship is the process of learning to follow Jesus Christ as Savior and Lord, seeking to observe all that Jesus commanded, by the power of the Holy Spirit and to the glory of God the Father.	3.0	2.7
Discipleship is the process of transformation that changes us to be increasingly more like Christ through the Word, the Spirit, and circumstance.	3.4	3.1
Discipleship is the process where a person purposely joins God to increasingly follow and live like Jesus, through the scriptures, the Holy Spirit, and the input of others.	3.6	3.0
Discipleship is becoming more and more like Jesus and letting Him live His life more and more in me.	3.6	3.6
Discipleship is about connecting with someone who will help you connect with God for the purpose of fulfilling your God-given destiny.	4.5	4.6

SCRIPTURE-SHAPED DISCIPLESHIP

The following are scripture passages cited by educators and exemplar church leaders as essential to their understanding of discipleship. All quotes are from the *New Living Translation* (NLT).

MATTHEW 4:19
Jesus called out to them, "Come, follow me, and I will show you how to fish for people!"

MATTHEW 28:18-20
Jesus came and told his disciples, "I have been given all authority in heaven and on earth. Therefore, go and make disciples of all the nations, baptizing them in the name of the Father and the Son and the Holy Spirit. Teach these new disciples to obey all the commands I have given you. And be sure of this: I am with you always, even to the end of the age."

JOHN 15:8-9
"When you produce much fruit, you are my true disciples. This brings great glory to my Father. I have loved you even as the Father has loved me. Remain in my love."

JOHN 17
Jesus looked up to heaven and said, "Father, the hour has come. Glorify your Son so he can give glory back to you. For you have given him authority over everyone. He gives eternal life to each one you have given him. And this is the way to have eternal life—to know you, the only true God, and Jesus Christ, the one you sent to earth. I brought glory to you here on earth by completing the work you gave me to do. Now, Father, bring me into the glory we shared before the world began.

"I have revealed you to the ones you gave me from this world. They were always yours. You gave them to me, and they have kept your word. Now they know that everything I have is a gift from you, for I have passed on to them the message you gave me. They accepted it and know that I came from you, and they believe you sent me.

"My prayer is not for the world, but for those you have given me, because they belong to you. All who are mine belong to you, and you have given them to me, so they bring me glory. Now I am departing from the world; they are staying in this world, but I am coming to you. Holy Father, you have given me your name; now protect them by the power of your name so that they will be united just as we are. During my time here, I protected them by the power of the name you gave me. I guarded them so that not one was lost, except the one headed for destruction, as the Scriptures foretold.

"Now I am coming to you. I told them many things while I was with them in this world so they would be filled with my joy. I have given them your word. And the world hates them because they do not belong to the world, just as I do not belong to the world. I'm not asking you to take them out of the world, but to keep them safe from the evil one. They do not belong to this world any more than I do. Make them holy by your truth; teach them your word, which is truth. Just as you sent me into the world, I am sending them into the world. And I give myself as a holy sacrifice for them so they can be made holy by your truth.

"I am praying not only for these disciples but also for all who will ever believe in me through their message. I pray that they will all be one, just as you and I are one—as you are in me, Father, and I am in you. And may they be in us so that the world will believe you sent me.

"I have given them the glory you gave me, so they may be one as we are one. I am in them and you are in me. May they experience such perfect unity that the world will know that you sent me and that you love them as much as you love me. Father, I want these whom you have given me to be with me where I am. Then they can see all the glory you gave me because you loved me even before the world began!

"O righteous Father, the world doesn't know you, but I do; and these disciples know you sent me. I have revealed you to them, and I will continue to do so. Then your love for me will be in them, and I will be in them."

ACTS 2:42-47

All the believers devoted themselves to the apostles' teaching, and to fellowship, and to sharing in meals (including the Lord's Supper), and to prayer.

> "O righteous Father, the world doesn't know you, but I do; and these disciples know you sent me."

A deep sense of awe came over them all, and the apostles performed many miraculous signs and wonders. And all the believers met together in one place and shared everything they had. They sold their property and possessions and shared the money with those in need. They worshiped together at the Temple each day, met in homes for the Lord's Supper, and shared their meals with great joy and generosity—all the while praising God and enjoying the goodwill of all the people. And each day the Lord added to their fellowship those who were being saved.

1 CORINTHIANS 4:15-17

For even if you had ten thousand others to teach you about Christ, you have only one spiritual father. For I became your father in Christ Jesus when I preached the Good News to you. So I urge you to imitate me.

That's why I have sent Timothy, my beloved and faithful child in the Lord. He will remind you of how I follow Christ Jesus, just as I teach in all the churches wherever I go.

1 CORINTHIANS 11:11

But among the Lord's people, women are not independent of men, and men are not independent of women.

PHILIPPIANS 4:6-7

Don't worry about anything; instead, pray about everything. Tell God what you need, and thank him for all he has done. Then you will experience God's peace, which exceeds anything we can understand. His peace will guard your hearts and minds as you live in Christ Jesus.

COLOSSIANS 1:28-29

So we tell others about Christ, warning everyone and teaching everyone with all the wisdom God has given us. We want to present them to God, perfect in their relationship to Christ. That's why I work and struggle so hard, depending on Christ's mighty power that works within me.

1 THESSALONIANS 2:3-13

You can see we were not preaching with any deceit or impure motives or trickery.

For we speak as messengers approved by God to be entrusted with the Good News. Our purpose is to please God, not people. He alone examines the motives of our hearts. Never once did we try to win you with flattery, as you well know. And God is our witness that we were not pretending to be your friends just to get your money! As for human praise, we have never sought it from you or anyone else.

As apostles of Christ we certainly had a right to make some demands of you, but instead we were like children among you. Or we were like a mother feeding and caring for her own children. We loved you so much that we shared with you not only God's Good News but our own lives, too.

Don't you remember, dear brothers and sisters, how hard we worked among you? Night and day we toiled to earn a living so that we would not be a burden to any of you as we preached God's Good News to you. You yourselves are our witnesses—and so is God—that we were devout and honest and faultless toward all of you believers. And you know that we treated each of you as a father treats his own children. We pleaded with you, encouraged you, and urged you to live your lives in a way that God would consider worthy. For he called you to share in his Kingdom and glory.

Therefore, we never stop thanking God that when you received his message from us, you didn't think of our words as mere human ideas. You accepted what we said as the very word of God—which, of course, it is. And this word continues to work in you who believe.

2 TIMOTHY 2:2

You have heard me teach things that have been confirmed by many reliable witnesses. Now teach these truths to other trustworthy people who will be able to pass them on to others.

2 TIMOTHY 3:16

All Scripture is inspired by God and is useful to teach us what is true and to make us realize what is wrong in our lives. It corrects us when we are wrong and teaches us to do what is right.

HEBREWS 10:24-25

Let us think of ways to motivate one another to acts of love and good works. And let us not neglect our meeting together, as some people do, but encourage one another, especially now that the day of his return is drawing near.

> Let us think of ways to motivate one another to acts of love and good works.

Are People Growing?

OF CHRISTIANS SAY THEY ARE ALMOST TO WHERE THEY WANT TO BE IN THEIR SPIRITUAL LIFE

OF CHRISTIANS SAY THEY ARE HAPPY WITH WHERE THEY ARE IN THEIR SPIRITUAL LIFE

HAVE YOU MADE PROGRESS IN YOUR SPIRITUAL GROWTH IN THE PAST YEAR?

● PRACTICING CHRISTIANS   ● NON-PRACTICING CHRISTIANS

| A LOT | SOME | A LOT | SOME |

TOP 3 REASONS CHRISTIANS WANT TO GROW SPIRITUALLY

I DESIRE TO KNOW JESUS, OR GOD, MORE

IT'S IMPORTANT TO BE IMPROVING OR GROWING IN ALL THINGS

I DESIRE TO BE MORE LIKE JESUS

2.
SPIRITUAL HEALTH

DISCIPLESHIP EFFECTIVENESS

How are churches doing when it comes to discipleship?

Christian adults believe their churches are doing well: 52 percent of those who have attended church in the past six months say their church "definitely does a good job helping people grow spiritually" and another 40 percent say it "probably" does so. Additionally, two-thirds of Christians who have attended church in the past six months *and* consider spiritual growth very or somewhat important say their church places "a lot" of emphasis on spiritual growth (67%); another 27 percent say their church gives "some" emphasis.

Church leaders give lower marks. Only 1 percent say "today's churches are doing very well at discipling new and young believers." A sizable majority—six in 10—feels that churches are discipling "not too well" (60%). Looking at their own church, 8 percent say they are doing "very well" and 56 percent "somewhat well at discipling new and young believers." Thus, pastors give their own church higher marks than churches overall, but few believe churches—their own or in general—are excelling in this area.

Leaders in non-mainline churches report doing better at discipleship (59% "somewhat well" and 8% "very well") than do leaders of mainline churches (46% "somewhat well" and 7% "very well"). Likewise, leaders of mostly non-white congregations are more likely to say they are doing "very well" (16%) than pastors and ministry leaders of majority white faith communities (6%).

ONLY 1 PERCENT OF CHURCH LEADERS SAY TODAY'S CHURCHES ARE DOING VERY WELL AT DISCIPLING NEW AND YOUNG BELIEVERS.

Not surprisingly, emphasis on discipleship is correlated with higher faith engagement. Three-quarters of practicing Christians, who have attended church in the past month and consider their faith very important, say their church places "a lot" of emphasis on spiritual growth (73%), while only 40 percent of non-practicing Christians say the same. Discipleship may be a driver of more active faith, or perhaps those already inclined to be more active in their faith are drawn to churches with a heavier emphasis on discipleship. Whatever the causal relationship, there is a clear need for more effective discipleship among Christians who are less active in their faith.

PARTICIPATION

Despite believing that their church emphasizes spiritual growth, only 20 percent[1] of Christian adults are involved in some sort of discipleship activity (attending Sunday school or fellowship group, meeting with a spiritual mentor, studying the Bible with a group, or reading and discussing a Christian book with a group). Practicing Christians (26%) who say spiritual growth is important are more likely to be involved than non-practicing Christians (7%) who say the same.

1. *These questions were only asked among Christians who say spiritual growth is very or somewhat important, but this percent represents the proportion among all Christians.*

Navigators alumni practice more active and rich spiritual disciplines, even compared with practicing Christians. The vast majority regularly pray (94%), study the Bible on their own (94%), meditate on Scripture (88%) and attend worship (94%). Most also are engaged in some form of interactive discipleship, whether small groups (Bible study 69%, book study 47%) or mentorship (53%). Historically, nearly all (94%) have been in a one-on-one mentoring relationship; 88 percent were in a Christian group in high school; and 84 percent participated in such a group during their college years.

Church leaders' estimates of their members' involvement in discipleship activities vary widely: Equal proportions estimate 15 percent or less and 75 percent or more of their congregations. Leaders' median estimate is 40 percent. Discipleship leaders are somewhat more optimistic than senior pastors, with most estimating about half of their members are involved in discipleship (50%). Both leader groups guess that a typical church member spends three hours per week (median) doing something to further their spiritual growth.

ESTIMATES OF MEMBER INVOLVEMENT IN DISCIPLESHIP ACTIVITIES
% among church leaders

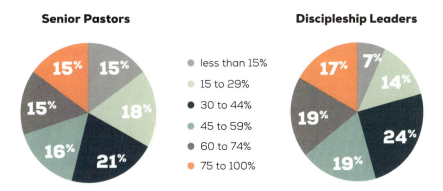

Among exemplar churches, estimates are slightly better. Typically, more than half of church members are involved in some sort of discipleship group or relationship. Exemplar leaders estimate that congregants spend an average of two to three hours per week (outside of church) devoted to spiritual development.

SPIRITUAL GROWTH

How do these investments in discipleship affect the spiritual health of Christians today? Most practicing Christians feel they have made "a lot" (40%) or "some" (51%) progress in their personal spiritual growth in the past year. By comparison, one in five non-practicing Christians has made "a lot" (20%) and 43 percent "some" progress. Those currently involved in at least one discipleship activity (attending Sunday school or fellowship group, meeting with a spiritual mentor, studying the Bible with a group, or reading and discussing a Christian book with a group) track closely with practicing Christians: 37 percent say they have made "a lot" and 57 percent "some" progress in their personal spiritual growth in the past year.

Perhaps not surprisingly, considering their level of investment in discipleship activities, 100 percent of Navigators alumni are satisfied with their spiritual life. Nearly all (94%) consider it "very important" to see progress in their spiritual life. Their continuing commitment has resulted in 43 percent making "a lot" of spiritual progress in the past year, and another 53 percent making "some progress."

Thirty-eight percent of Christian adults say they are "happy with where they are in their spiritual life" and another 36 percent are "almost to where they want to be." In this case, more practicing Christians (39%) than non-practicing (30%) are "almost" where they want to be with respect to spiritual growth, indicating an ongoing attention to spiritual health. Indeed, three-quarters of practicing Christians (77%) but only 37 percent of non-practicing Christians believe it is "very important to see growth in their spiritual life." Non-practicing Christians are more likely to consider spiritual growth "somewhat important" (42% vs. 20% of practicing Christians).

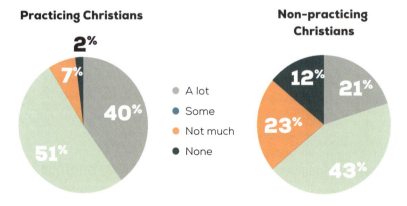

PERSONAL SPIRITUAL PROGRESS: PAST 12 MONTHS
% among Christians

The two groups also report different motivations for seeking spiritual growth. Practicing Christians are most motivated by "a general desire to know Jesus, or God, more" (46%); "a general desire to be more like Jesus" (41%); and "the Bible instructs us to be more like Jesus" (34%). Non-practicing Christians, on the other hand, say they "think it is important to be improving or growing in general/in all things" (51%); "have been through a lot, and growing spiritually will help me" (41%); and "have a general desire to know Jesus, or God, more" (36%).

Why do Navigators alumni pursue spiritual growth? They align with the organization's mission "to know Christ and make Him known" and with the most common definition of discipleship: "becoming more Christ-like." Eighty-two percent of alumni say they desire to be more like Jesus, and nearly as many (78%) desire to know Him more. Half simply feel compelled by the Holy Spirit to grow (51%).

In addition to being personally spiritually healthy, those discipled by The Navigators want to have an impact on the people around them. They are evangelists, with three-quarters desiring to have an impact on friends (78%) and relatives (76%), and even more wanting their faith to impact the world around them (their community, 84%; society, 78%).

REASONS FOR SPIRITUAL GROWTH

Q: There are a lot of different reasons people desire to grow spiritually. Out of the following list, please tell me which you consider the top two or three most important reasons that you want to grow spiritually.

	All Christians	Practicing Christians	Non-practicing Christians	Navigators Alumni
I have a general desire to know Jesus, or God, more	43%	46%	36%	78%
I think it is important to be improving or growing in general / in all things	39	33	51	6
I have a general desire to be more like Jesus	35	41	25	82
I have been through a lot, and growing spiritually will help me	31	26	41	2
The Bible instructs us to be more like Jesus	29	34	18	33
I feel compelled by the Holy Spirit	28	33	19	51
My church encourages spiritual growth	20	24	12	2
I am inspired by other people, and want to be more like them	13	12	15	16
I feel pressure from other Christians	2	1	3	0

Q&A WITH MIKE JORDAHL

Q: When you look at practicing Christians' main motivations for spiritual growth (to become more like Jesus) compared to non-practicing Christians (it's important to improve/grow in all things), how do you think these different motivations affect people's pursuit of or prioritizing of discipleship?

A: In Psalm 27:4 David says, "One thing I ask of the Lord, this is what I seek: that I may dwell in the house of the Lord all the days of my life, to gaze upon the beauty of the Lord and to seek him in his temple." David was asking God to allow him to be in his presence. More than anything else, David said, he wanted to be with the Lord.

We can learn a lot from David's focus. David did not say, "These many things I dabble at." No, he was a man with focus and his focus was on desiring and being with the Lord.

Jesus said the same thing several times, including in Matthew 6:33: "Seek first the kingdom of God and his righteousness and all these things will be added to you." Jesus wanted us to seek God's kingdom above all else. This leads me to pray often for myself "Lord, help me seek your kingdom (your rule in me)—and to seek you yourself above all else."

Some who profess faith in Christ have the erroneous belief that just because they went through a Christian ritual at some point, or because they had a season of truly seeking God, that they are "set for life." Others think showing up at a church service once in a while is all they need. And some, in their pursuit of many things, miss out on the one big thing of truly following Jesus.

Helping non-practicing Christians yearn for and learn to cultivate a passion to know Christ is one of the biggest challenges facing the Body of Christ today. Hopefully, the research and findings in this book will help us all move forward in proactively accomplishing this task.

MIKE JORDAHL and his wife, Nancy, have served with The Navigators in Iowa, Kansas, New England and Colorado. Mike previously served for six years as the U.S. Collegiate Director for The Navigators. Today he serves on the Leadership Team of The Navigators 20s Mission and as the National Director of CityLife. Mike is passionate about empowering men and women in their 20s to live intentional and missional lives rooted in a vibrant relationship with God.

Q&A WITH MIKE JORDAHL (CONTINUED)

Q: Practicing Christians are, not surprisingly, much more likely to participate in any discipleship activity (such as Sunday school, Bible reading, or a mentor relationship). This seems to illustrate a real need for helping those Christians who are not currently attending church to engage in these activities. How are The Navigators specifically poised and equipped to reach out to these Christians outside the walls of the church?

A: We know the statistic – just about 20% of all adults in the U.S. attend any kind of church on a given weekend. A similar percentage of adults never attend a church. And then, there is the 60% in the middle – those who rarely or only occasionally participate in a church service.

What can we do to reach and disciple all these people?

In John 1:14 we read, "The Word became flesh and made his dwelling among us" (*NIV*). *The Message* says it more graphically, "The Word became flesh and blood, and moved into the neighborhood."

The New Testament reality is that God himself did not beckon people to meet him in a certain place. Instead, he became one of us! In essence, he came to us, became one of us and met us—with his message—on our turf.

This model of relational ministry is at the heart of The Navigators' approach. Navigators go to and live among people right where they are: where they work, live, play and study.

NavNeighbors and Navs Workplace are just two examples of ministries that focus on empower-ing and equipping believers to reach out to and disciple others in the context of where they are. We find again and again that men and women who never or rarely go to a church are eager and willing to read the Bible, talk about God and begin to seek him on their own turf.

Perhaps the great challenge of our day is to equip believers everywhere to reach and disciple people in the good news of Christ in the living rooms, boardrooms, pool halls, street corners and happy hours of our culture.

Q: Why do you think it might be important to focus efforts on these non-practicing Christians? And what are some activities or places in which to do that?

A: Casual followers of Christ are nothing new. Jesus had a lot of them in his day. We recognize them as the "multitudes" or "crowds" in the Gospels. On the one hand, Jesus clearly welcomed these casual followers, declaring to them "If anyone is thirsty, let him come to me and drink" (John 7:37).

On the other hand, Jesus consistently called these crowds to go beyond being his casual followers: "Large crowds were traveling with Jesus, and turning to them he said: 'If anyone comes to me and does not hate his father and mother, his wife and children, his brothers and sisters—yes, even his own life—he cannot be my disciple. And anyone who does not carry his cross and follow me cannot be my disciple'" (Luke 14:25).

Many new believers have a passion to live for Christ but they don't always know what to do to live out that passion. Without help to grow as a disciple they slowly drift into the realm of casually or barely following Jesus.

What can we do to address this? Personal disciplemaking is essential if we are to see masses of casual followers of Christ become his committed followers.

Although I had a regular diet of church services and sermons, my faith didn't noticeably deepen until Barry, a college senior involved with The Navigators, began to spend personal time with me. We did Bible study together, shared our faith with others and he began to help me practically live as a committed follower of Christ. He began to disciple me.

And, as friends of mine began to put their faith in Christ, Barry and others taught me how to personally disciple them.

Churches will be well served to encourage mature followers of Christ to actively engage in sharing their faith with the people around them and in intentionally discipling new and casual believers.

Q: How might Navigators encourage or aid pastors in the discipleship work their churches are doing?

A: Many churches today have one or more Navigators sitting in their pews. These are laymen and laywomen who at some point in their lives were personally discipled to follow Christ and who received some level of training in how to reach out to and disciple others.

We repeatedly hear from these people that they are asked to serve in their local churches through jobs like teaching, ushering, taking care of babies, ministering to students and shut-ins and sitting on committees.

But they are rarely encouraged to use their Nav training by making time to reach out to their neighbors or co-workers with the gospel. And rarely are their outreach and disciplemaking efforts in their natural contexts celebrated by their pastor or local church.

Here are three things a pastor can do to increase the disciplemaking efforts in their church:

1. If you have never experienced it, ask someone you trust to disciple you. Of course, this takes humility, but if your training consists primarily of classroom learning, you might actually benefit from the arm-around-the-shoulder approach of someone who can help you walk not only as a pastor but as a committed follower of Christ. (Many Navigators staff have discreetly discipled a pastor. To see if there are Navigators staff in your area, visit www.navigators.org/FindStaff.)

2. Do all you can to free those in your church with discipleship training to practice what they have learned in their natural contexts—and to pass it on to others.

3. If you are interested in considering a program to transform your whole church into a disciplemaking church, contact Navigator Church Ministries at LifelongLaborers@navigators.org.

What Is Working?

HOW DO CHRISTIANS WANT TO BE DISCIPLED?

(AMONG THE 9 IN 10 CHRISTIANS WHO SAY SPIRITUAL GROWTH IS IMPORTANT)

- ON MY OWN
- WITH A GROUP
- ONE-ON-ONE
- MIX OF GROUP + ONE-ON-ONE

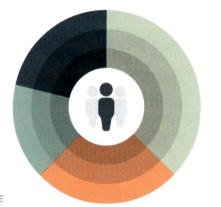
 37%
 25%
 16%
 21%

1 IN 3 CHRISTIANS IS LOOKING FOR ONE-ON-ONE DISCIPLESHIP.

1 IN 4 CHRISTIANS IS CURRENTLY BEING DISCIPLED BY SOMEONE.

1 IN 5 IS DISCIPLING SOMEONE ELSE.

I BELIEVE MY SPIRITUAL LIFE HAS AN IMPACT ON …

RELATIVES 37% — FRIENDS 36%

COMMUNITY 33% — SOCIETY 29%

I BELIEVE MY SPIRITUAL LIFE IS ENTIRELY PRIVATE

29%

WHO HAS THE MOST IMPACT ON YOUR SPIRITUAL JOURNEY?

1. FAMILY MEMBERS
2. PEOPLE AT CHURCH
3. BIBLE STUDY OR SMALL GROUP
4. FRIENDS
5. A MENTOR
6. CHRISTIAN COMMUNITY OTHER THAN CHURCH
7. ONLINE SOCIAL NETWORKS

WHAT HAS BEEN MOST HELPFUL FOR YOUR SPIRITUAL JOURNEY?

1. REGULAR PRAYER
2. ATTENDING CHURCH
3. QUIET TIME
4. PERSONAL BIBLE STUDY
5. GROUP BIBLE STUDY
6. MEDITATING ON SCRIPTURE
7. A SPIRITUAL MENTOR

3.
DISCIPLESHIP MODELS

GROUP VS. ONE-ON-ONE VS. INDIVIDUAL

Christian adults are split on their preferences when it comes to models of discipleship: small group, one-on-one or individual (solitary) format.

Among the nine out of 10 Christians who say spiritual growth is important (90%), it's notable that more than one-third say they prefer to pursue spiritual growth on their own (37%). Similarly, two in five of all Christian adults consider their spiritual life "entirely private" (41%). This is a greater proportion—though only slightly—than Christians who believe their faith, rather than being private, has an impact on relatives (37%), friends (36%) and their community (33%).

The pluralities that prefer solitary spiritual pursuit are worrisome for long-term spiritual health. Exemplar testimony and data presented elsewhere in this study show the centrality of relationships to transformational discipleship.

Navigators alumni believe discipleship is relational. They prefer small group (49%) and a mix of the models (45%). Accordingly, half are engaged in a mentoring relationship: 51 percent are discipling others and 43 percent are being discipled.

Thirty-five percent of Christian adults who say spiritual growth is important report that their church recommends meeting with a spiritual mentor; 50 percent of their churches recommend studying the Bible with a group; and 50 percent recommend studying the Bible independently. These are not exclusive preferences but, generally speaking, the proportions align with Christians' preferences for discipleship methods.

SHOULD SPIRITUAL LIFE BE PRIVATE OR PUBLIC?

Q: Some people see their spiritual life as entirely private; other people consider their personal spiritual life relevant to other people. Do you consider your personal spiritual life to be... (Multiple response)

(% among those who feel spiritual growth is at least somewhat important)

	All Christians	Practicing Christians	Non-practicing Christians	Navigators Alumni
Entirely private	41%	28%	60%	0%
Having an impact on relatives	37	46	24	76
Having an impact on friends	36	47	19	78
Having an impact on your community	33	44	15	84
Having an impact on society	29	38	15	78
Other	10	12	8	22

Among the 90 percent of Christian adults who believe spiritual growth is important, one-quarter prefers a small-group setting for discipleship (25%). Another one in five prefers a combination of group and one-on-one discipleship (21%) and 16 percent prefer one-on-one only. Thus, in total, about one-third of those pursuing spiritual growth like to include some element of one-on-one discipleship.

Not all of those who prefer discipleship "pairs" are currently involved in a one-on-one discipleship relationship: Out of the nine in 10 Christian adults who believe spiritual growth is important, 23 percent are currently being discipled by somone (29% of practicing vs. 12% of non-practicing Christians), and 19 percent are discipling someone else (25% of practicing vs. 9% of non-practicing Christians).

PREFERRED METHOD OF DISCIPLESHIP

% among Christians who say spiritual growth is very or somewhat important

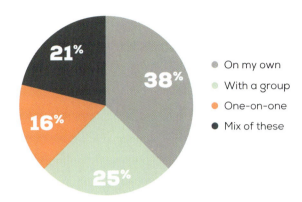

- On my own — 38%
- With a group — 25%
- One-on-one — 16%
- Mix of these — 21%

Interestingly, Christian adults who have previously been involved in a college ministry (32%) are more likely to currently be in a one-on-one discipleship relationship. Forty percent of those currently being discipled were once in a college ministry. By comparison, 31 percent of those *not* being discipled were in a college ministry. Forty-five percent of those currently discipling someone else were once in a college ministry, compared with 30 percent of those *not* currently discipling someone part of a college ministry.

One-on-one discipleship relationships are established in various ways: Of those currently being discipled by another person, one quarter say that person invited them (27%); one in five invited their mentor (20%); and about one quarter were paired by the church (23%)—but the largest proportion, 28 percent, were matched "some other way."

Attitudes towards relationships that impact spiritual journeys suggest that family, people at church, small groups, friends and mentors are most valuable to Christians' spiritual growth. Online social networks have the least (but some) impact.

THE PLURALITIES OF CHRISTIAN ADULTS WHO PREFER SOLITARY SPIRITUAL PURSUIT ARE WORRISOME FOR LONG-TERM SPIRITUAL HEALTH.

MOST VALUABLE RELATIONSHIPS TO CHRISTIANS' SPIRITUAL JOURNEYS

% among Christians who say spiritual growth is at least somewhat important

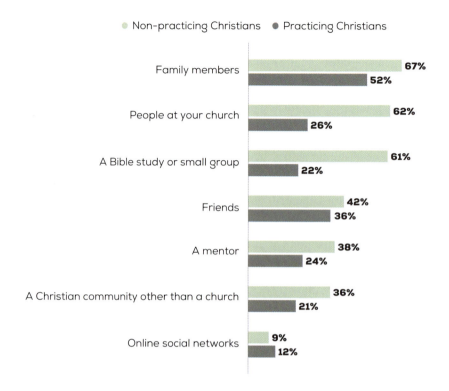

● Non-practicing Christians   ● Practicing Christians

Relationship	Non-practicing	Practicing
Family members	67%	52%
People at your church	62%	26%
A Bible study or small group	61%	22%
Friends	42%	36%
A mentor	38%	24%
A Christian community other than a church	36%	21%
Online social networks	9%	12%

When forced to choose the single method of discipleship they believe is most effective, church leaders select small group formats (52%) nearly two-to-one over discipleship pairs (29%). Mainline pastors (71%) are even more likely than non-mainline pastors (47%) to consider small groups most effective, and non-mainline leaders place a higher priority on one-on-one discipleship relationships compared with mainline leaders (32% vs. 16%, respectively). However, fewer non-mainline leaders prefer discipleship pairs than small groups.

When considering the proportion of Christian adults who prefer a mix of group and one-on-one discipleship, the overall split between these two methods is comparable to that of church leaders. However, the greatest disconnect between leaders and their congregants is the perceived utility of solitary study for spiritual growth. Just one in nine leaders considers this method most effective (11%), compared with 37 percent of Christian adults who prefer private study.

Preferences are similar among exemplar churches. A portion of exemplar leaders prefers the mature-to-new believer relationship, usually one-on-one. More use *both* this approach and the peer-to-peer/small group model, which is believed to be more appealing to members. Exemplars widely consider a one-on-one component—whether Bible study or just conversation—essential to fruitful discipleship. Only two among 37 exemplar respondents report using the peer/small group format on its own.

Do church leaders take their own advice when it comes to discipleship? Somewhat. Fully 94 percent are currently discipling at least one other Christian. However, only six in 10 are being discipled themselves (62%). Discipleship leaders (72%) are somewhat more likely than senior pastors (59%) to have a spiritual mentor, and these relationships are more common in larger churches: Eight out of 10 church leaders of 500+ member churches are being discipled (78%), compared with 64 percent of those with 100 to 499 members and 55 percent of those who lead in churches with fewer than 100 members.

"People are too busy with church stuff that is less important—a matter of good overriding the best."

Christian educator

MOST EFFECTIVE METHOD OF DISCIPLESHIP

% among church leaders

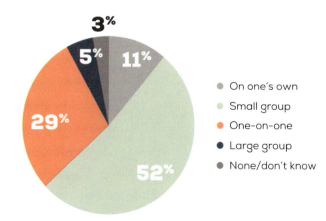

- On one's own — 11%
- Small group — 52%
- One-on-one — 29%
- Large group — 5%
- None/don't know — 3%

PREFERRED METHOD OF DISCIPLESHIP

Q: Which of the following is your most preferred method for discipleship?
(% among those who feel spiritual growth is at least somewhat important)

	All Christians	Practicing Christians	Non-practicing Christians	Navigators Alumni
On your own	37%	30%	53%	4%
With a group	25	29	17	49
One-on-one with another person	16	18	13	2
A mix of these	21	23	16	45

INVOLVEMENT IN DISCIPLESHIP / PERSONAL MENTORING

Discipleship Relationships	All Church Leaders	Senior Pastors	Discipleship Leaders	All Christians	Practicing Christians	Non-practicing Christians	Navigators Alumni
Personally active in discipling members of your church /others	94%	94%	95%	19%	25%	9%	51%
Personally being discipled by someone else	62	59	72	23	29	12	43

SPIRITUAL DISCIPLINES & ACTIVITIES

According to pastors, the most critical elements of discipleship are matters of the heart rather than of structure. Aside from prayer and time with God, the top three spiritual disciplines pastors believe are essential to discipleship are "personal commitment to grow in Christlikeness" (94%), "attending a local church" (91%) and "a deep love for God" (90%). Having "a comprehensive discipleship curriculum" is by far the least important element of effective discipleship according to pastors, 44 percent of whom select it as essential.

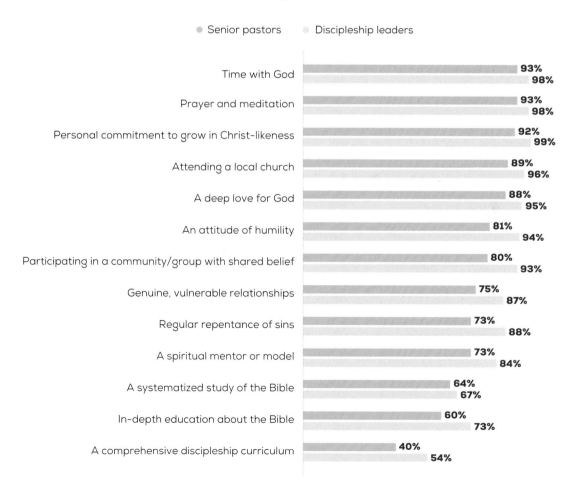

ESSENTIAL ELEMENTS OF DISCIPLESHIP
% among church leaders

● Senior pastors   ● Discipleship leaders

Element	Senior pastors	Discipleship leaders
Time with God	93%	98%
Prayer and meditation	93%	98%
Personal commitment to grow in Christ-likeness	92%	99%
Attending a local church	89%	96%
A deep love for God	88%	95%
An attitude of humility	81%	94%
Participating in a community/group with shared belief	80%	93%
Genuine, vulnerable relationships	75%	87%
Regular repentance of sins	73%	88%
A spiritual mentor or model	73%	84%
A systematized study of the Bible	64%	67%
In-depth education about the Bible	60%	73%
A comprehensive discipleship curriculum	40%	54%

HELPFUL RESOURCES FOR SPIRITUAL GROWTH:
CHRISTIAN ADULTS

Q: Which ones have been most helpful for your own spiritual journey?
(% among those who have used each)

	All Christians	Navigators Alumni
Regular prayer	59%	57%
Attending church worship services	55	27
Quiet time	40	78
Studying the Bible on your own	38	63
Studying the Bible with a group	31	65
Meditating on Scripture	25	61
Meeting with a spiritual mentor	24	84
Attending Sunday school or fellowship group	22	18
Listening to Christian music	22	16
A Bible study curriculum	19	22
Reading and discussing a Christian book with a group	14	16
Scripture memorization	11	61
Podcasts about the Bible or Christian life	10	16
A Christian student group in college	9	53
A Christian student group in high school	6	6

Christian adults, by contrast, say the basics—prayer and attending church services—have been most helpful in their own spiritual journey. Among Christian adults who report ever having used these methods, 59 percent say "regular prayer" and 55 percent say "attending church worship services" have been most helpful. In contrast, three in 10 Christians have been part of a Bible study small group and consider it most helpful in their spiritual development (31%), and one-quarter have had a spiritual mentor and consider this relationship most helpful (24%).

The disparity between church leaders' and Christian adults' perceptions of what is most effective for spiritual growth may represent the tension between the ideal approach and what actually occurs in practice. Alternately or additionally, some Christians may be simply less self-aware about their spiritual condition.

Personal Bible study (92%), small group Bible study (88%) and one-on-one discussions with mature believers (83%) are considered by church leaders to have the most significant impact on developing disciples. Listening to media is considered least effective (45%).

Among Christian adults, 35 percent are currently *only* using some sort of non-personal discipleship (podcasts or listening to music).

METHODS OF DISCIPLESHIP THAT MAKE SIGNIFICANT IMPACT:
CHURCH LEADERS

Q: Among each of the following methods for spiritual growth, which do you think will have a significant impact on developing disciples?
(Multiple responses allowed)

	All Church Leaders
Personal Bible study	92%
Small group Bible study	88
Regular one-on-one conversations about discipleship issues with a more mature believer	83
Teaching the Word in weekly services	81
One-on-one study with a more mature believer	76
Memorizing Scripture	65
Reading Christian books and publications	58
Listening to media (i.e radio, podcasts, recorded sermons)	45

▶ Q&A WITH LINDY BLACK

LINDY BLACK has been on staff with the Navigators for 34 years. She currently serves as the Associate U.S. Director, with a focus on bringing support and leadership capacity to the U.S. Director, Doug Nuenke, and the three U.S. Field Directors. She also oversees staff development teams. Lindy has served as a member of the National Leadership Team since October 2010. She lives in Colorado Springs with her husband of 37 years.

Q: In the research, people express a desire for one-on-one mentoring relationships—yet also admitted these relationships are hard to get into. How can Navigators help bridge this gap between mentors and those looking to be mentored?

A: Navigators are well equipped with tools to be used as needed. They in turn can help others develop toolboxes. Begin with a few areas—for example, how to help someone have motivation and a plan for a consistent quiet time over the next three months. And as a person grows in confidence, they can add more resources or tools. With time, you will be able to improvise or adapt to the needs of a particular person. As a mentor steps out in faith and offers what they have experienced, they can understand how to make practical discipleship reproducible.

A suggestion to those looking for mentors – ask yourself what you enjoy or have a real desire to grow in (for example, reading the Bible, sharing your faith, memorizing Scripture) and look for someone who is modeling in this area and invite them to help you further develop. Often we go to an area we are very weak and unmotivated and think this is where we need help. Most of us learn by doing. Doing with others who can share their lives multiplies the impact!

Q: What gets in the way of personal discipleship and disciple-making as a ministry activity?

A: When the goal becomes doing, we can quickly become self-focused. Discipleship is knowing and becoming like Christ—living in vibrant, fruitful relationship with him. What we do (personally or with others) is to be a means, not the end. We read the Scriptures to know him—not to make ourselves more acceptable to him. We pray to seek and know his heart—not to manipulate or impress the Lord. Even disciple-making can become a project or activity in and of itself rather than a privileged participation in the work of the Lord.

Q: In the research, leaders often express a need for discipleship to be organic and not programmatic. How do The Navigators take advantage of programs, systems and structures without getting tangled up or bogged down in them?

A: The strength of programs and systems is often in providing a beginning point and concrete steps to a greater end. The Navigators utilize time-tested programs like the Topical Memory System or the 2:7 series to incorporate spiritual disciplines and give mentors tools for discipling other. We have numerous Bible studies published through NavPress that give structure to digging in to the Word. Developing discipleship plans gives direction to enable intentional building into another person's life. These are means to knowing Christ and making him known, and helping others do the same.

Q: What is helpful (and what is unhelpful) in the onboarding process for discipling relationships?

A: It's important to define expectations. Sometimes people are looking for friendship more than intentional input, but they ask to be discipled. You need to clarify how often you will meet and why you will meet. It is usually good to set an initial timeframe (like two to three months) and then re-evaluate. It's important to agree on how long your commitment is, how you will structure your time together and how long your meetings will last, as well as what you will prepare (or not prepare) ahead of time. It's critical to ask and answer the question, "What do we hope to see from this relationship?"

Q: Aside from one-on-one mentoring relationships, what other types of relational discipling have you seen be effective? What has made them effective?

A: God uses friendships of many kinds to bring an "iron sharpening iron" effect. Small-group Bible studies and discussion groups provide the opportunity for peer learning, motivation and encouragement. Pairs, trios or groups meeting for prayer often open the door to experience God through others and to grow in faith. Doing life together with others in a like season of life and faith can bring support and mutual strength. Beginning a new ministry outreach with several others (where you live, work or play) can be a great stretching and learning opportunity that leads to wisdom and maturity in the work of the Kingdom.

What Is Standing in the Way?

ONLY 1 IN 5 CHRISTIANS IS INVOLVED IN SOME SORT OF DISCIPLESHIP ACTIVITY

TOP BARRIERS TO SPIRITUAL GROWTH

● PRACTICING CHRISTIANS   ● NON-PRACTICING CHRISTIANS

   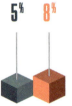  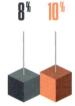

4% / 6%	5% / 6%	5% / 7%	5% / 8%	11% / 8%	8% / 10%
I HAVEN'T FOUND ANYONE WILLING TO HELP ME	IT'S HARD TO FIND GOOD RESOURCES OR INFORMATION	I DON'T KNOW WHERE TO START	MY FAMILY MEMBERS ARE NOT SUPPORTIVE	MY FRIENDS ARE NOT AS INTERESTED IN SPIRITUAL THINGS	I HAVE OTHER MORE IMPORTANT PRIORITIES RIGHT NOW

     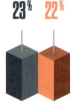

10% / 12%	16% / 13%	9% / 15%	9% / 16%	6% / 16%	23% / 22%
I DON'T WANT TO THINK ABOUT MISTAKES I'VE MADE IN THE PAST	SPIRITUAL GROWTH WILL REQUIRE A LOT OF HARD WORK	I DON'T WANT TO GET TOO PERSONAL WITH OTHER PEOPLE	I'VE HAD BAD PAST EXPERIENCES WITH GROUPS OR INDIVIDUALS	I CAN'T FIND A GOOD CHURCH OR CHRISTIAN COMMUNITY	GENERAL BUSYNESS OF LIFE

4.
OBSTACLES

All audiences interviewed—Christian adults, church leaders, exemplars and educators—agree on the most significant barrier to spiritual growth: the general "busyness" of life. However, church leaders and Christian adults disagree substantially on the *magnitude* of this barrier. Specifically, 85 percent of church leaders say busyness is a major obstacle to discipleship, while only 22 percent of practicing Christians say the same. Leaders are also concerned about an overall lack of commitment to discipleship.

None of the barriers presented as options to Christians resonate as a major obstacle with more than one-quarter of respondents. This lack of concern about barriers to spiritual growth mirrors Christians' overall satisfaction with "the basics"—that is, that attending worship services and spending time in prayer are the most helpful elements of their spiritual growth.

Further evidence of general spiritual apathy is the one in 10 self-identified Christians who says their spiritual growth is "not too" or "not at all" important. Two-thirds of these say they are comfortable with where they are spiritually. There is simply no drive to prioritize spiritual growth.

Church leaders see a great number of obstacles to healthy discipleship in their churches. Senior pastors and discipleship leaders believe that personal issues such as sinful habits (70%), pride that inhibits teachability (70%) and a lack of supportive relationships (55%) are significant barriers. A lack of qualified and willing discipleship leaders is also a major obstacle (59%).

Exemplars cite similar barriers, which they variously describe as a self-focused, consumerist approach to church; impatience, especially on the part of the disciple/younger Christian; and potential leaders feeling ill-equipped.

Few church leaders (18%) and practicing Christians (5%) cite a lack of resources as a major obstacle to spiritual growth. Exemplars go further, saying a process or format that is too prescriptive, or that takes up the time of leaders and members, are common and significant obstacles to effective discipleship.

> "[The biggest barrier is] spiritual navel gazing, which is particularly prevalent in the me-first society we live in."
>
> Exemplar church leader

MAJOR OBSTACLES TO DISCIPLESHIP:
CHURCH LEADERS

Q: There are various things that can get in the way of someone progressing as a disciple. I'm going to read a list of some of these things. For each one, tell me if you think it is a major obstacle, a minor obstacle, or not really an obstacle for people trying to grow as disciples today.

(% major obstacle)

	All Church Leaders	Senior Pastors	Discipleship Leaders
Lack of commitment	87%	86%	88%
Too much busyness in their lives	85	85	84
Sinful habits	70	69	75
Pride that inhibits teachability	70	68	74
Lack of qualified and willing "disciplers"	59	58	64
Lack of supportive relationships	55	53	60
Lack of strong leadership	53	50	61
Negative peer relationships	51	48	60
Lack of a model for discipleship	49	46	55
Fear of vulnerability	47	46	51
Guilt about things in their past	44	42	51
Lack of good resources	18	18	18

MAJOR OBSTACLES TO DISCIPLESHIP:
CHRISTIAN ADULTS

Q: Now switching gears, I'm going to ask about things that get in the way of your spiritual growth. For each item I read, tell me if this is a major obstacle, a minor obstacle, or not really an obstacle to your spiritual growth.

(% major obstacle)

	Practicing Christians	Non-practicing Christians
General busyness of life	23%	22%
Spiritual growth will require a lot of hard work	16	13
My friends are not as interested in spiritual things	11	8
Not wanting to think about mistakes you've made in the past	10	12
I have had bad past experiences with groups or individuals	9	16
Not wanting to get too personal with other people	9	15
I have other more important priorities right now	8	10
I can't find a good church or Christian community to join	6	16
My family members are not supportive	5	8
I would not, or do not, know where to start	5	7
It's hard to find good resources or information for spiritual growth	5	6
I haven't found anyone willing to help me grow spiritually	4	6

OBSTACLES TO ONE-ON-ONE DISCIPLESHIP

Evidence of spiritual disengagement emerges again when considering the barriers to individual, one-on-one discipleship. When asked why they are not being discipled by another believer, three in 10 Christian adults say they simply have not thought about it (29%), and one in seven says no one has suggested it (14%). A significant minority has thought about a mentor relationship but do not think they need to be discipled by another person (25%).

On the other hand, among the eight in 10 who do not currently disciple someone else (81%), three in 10 do not feel qualified or equipped (30%). This underscores church leaders' perceptions of a key barrier to discipleship: lack of qualified and willing "disciplers." Additional obstacles mirror the disengaged perspective of those not currently discipling someone else: 23 percent have not thought about it and 20 percent say no one has suggested they mentor another person.

Church leaders say the top barriers to mature believers discipling younger believers are "too much busyness in their lives" (65%) and "lack of commitment" (41%). Thirty-nine percent say "feelings of inadequacy" also hinder potential discipleship leaders.

These perspectives confirm that, overall, there are no major structural barriers hindering participation in discipleship in the Church today. Rather, a lack of priority—on the part of Christians *and* of churches—has produced weak investment in spiritual growth. Aside from potential disciplers feeling ill-equipped—which could be a factor of self confidence or of training, both of which are surmountable—all other reasons for non-participation point to apathy.

> "Most believers consider themselves inadequately trained, or ungifted to disciple another believer. Spiritual parenting is not promoted and modeled by the leadership in many churches. There is an assumption that the appropriation of biblical knowledge will by itself lead to spiritual maturity."
>
> Christian educator

THE SPIRITUAL LANDSCAPE HAS CHANGED

BY FRAN SCIACCA
AN EXCERPT FROM *SO, WHAT'S YOUR POINT*

I am a second-generation American, born of Sicilian immigrants. My grandparents' names are in the records on Ellis Island a half mile from the Statue of Liberty. Emma Lazarus's poem on the base of that statue is a historic invitation, especially to those who are poor and broken, that lies beneath our nation's diversity.

> *"Keep, ancient lands, your storied pomp!" cries she*
> *With silent lips. "Give me your tired, your poor,*
> *Your huddled masses yearning to breathe free.*

Recently, there has been no end to the rhetoric and dialogue about quotas and qualifications for crossing our borders. But while all the talking was taking place, an amazing shift quietly occurred. America's religious landscape shifted.

- The percentage of Americans calling themselves "Christian" has fallen since 1990 from 86 percent to 76 percent.

- Twenty-five percent of those aged eighteen and older have "no religious affiliation"; this number has *doubled* since those in this group were children.

- Only four percent of eighteen- to twenty-five-year-olds listed "becoming more spiritual" as their most important goal in life.

Mark Silk, professor of religion and public life at Trinity College in Hartford, Connecticut, puts it bluntly: "The real dirty little secret of religiosity in America is that there are so many people for whom spiritual interest, thinking about ultimate questions, is minimal."

Unfortunately, since the Sixties collapsed, the American church has simultaneously withdrawn from the public square and created a caricature of Christianity that resembles biblical faith less and less. It's not so much that U.S. Christianity is being secularized. Rather more subtly, Christianity is either degenerating or being displaced.

Without being simplistic, I think one can almost chart our migration from authenticity to paucity by decade.

In the church culture of the 1960s, "Christian" was an assumed synonym for "American." Christianity and democracy were presumed to be inseparable. Most of us in the counterculture were, I suspect, some threat to the American way of life. But we were no threat to the gospel. I believe the church, as an institution, lost much of its credibility with the rising generation during the 1960s thanks to a perceived (or perhaps real) attitude of self-righteousness.

The 1970s seemed to be a decade of the church's seeking to regain that lost credibility. It was a season of intense interest in apologetics and the Christian mind. Books by Francis Schaeffer, Os Guinness, Josh McDowell, James Warwick Montgomery, and others began to pour out of Christian publishing houses, demonstrating that a Christian can have a satisfied mind, not just a warm heart. But the decade was also a period of incredible accommodation to culture. There seemed to be a campaign to convince the watching world that they should take us seriously. This was a season when impressing the secular culture became the "point." We quietly traded a distinct biblical identity as individuals, and corporately as a community of faith, for a subcultural one. We began to see ourselves in *contrast* to the culture instead of in *comparison* with Scripture.

It should come as no surprise that the 1980s could be characterized as a decade of Christian narcissism. This intense season of "focus" was, tragically, directed primarily toward ourselves. A 1980s edition of *Current Christian Books* listed nearly five hundred titles that began with *How To*. Books promising sexual fulfillment in marriage, foolproof parenting, success in business, and personal happiness were commonplace. Professional Christian counseling services sprang up everywhere, as we sought to find, nurture, and heal our inner selves. The consequences were numerous and

> We began to see ourselves in *contrast* to the culture instead of in *comparison* with Scripture.

significant, but one stands out among the rest: A near complete retreat from cultural influence and concern. But that would soon change, or at least an attempt would be made to do so.

The 1990s became a decade defined by our attempts to retrieve what secular culture had "stolen" from us. Thanks to the rhetoric of several prominent Christian leaders, we wound up being "at war" with the culture. Christian activism was the theme of radio and TV talk shows, conferences, and books. The clarion call was for us to reclaim what had been taken from us as Americans and as Christians.

When you're wrapped up in yourself, you become a very small package indeed. Jesus said that the strong man's house couldn't be plundered unless he was tied up. I suspect that the plundering of "traditional values" happened because we *were* tied up—with our busyness. We were distracted, worshiping at the shrine of Self, in the name of Christ.

The thing that was relinquished during this period was a sense of *mission*. Those we found ourselves "at war" with were the very ones to whom we had been sent. The mandate to be ambassadors of Yahweh, committed to reconciling sinners, fell out of our spiritual backpack. In our zeal to heal ourselves, we had become poisoned by distraction. A commitment to issues replaced a burden for individuals. Politics had become more important than people. Leonard Sweet summarized our condition clearly: "The greatest sin of the Church today is not any sin of commission or sin of omission, but the sin of no mission."

I am deeply encouraged by the rising number of churches planting other churches, and the growing sensitivity to the need to have a reason—a purpose—for existing. And in an America whose spiritual landscape has been reordered by religious diversity and atrophy, learning to think "missionally" might be a good thing. But if it turns out to be the next hot thing for God's people, then being "missional" might be an attempt to fill a void *within*, not responding to a call from without.

FRAN SCIACCA is a veteran Bible teacher and author of over 30 books and Bible studies. He currently directs Hands of Hur (handsofhur.org), a unique Bible teaching ministry whose vision is to revitalize and strengthen the leaders of existing ministries, especially those serving in a collegiate environment.

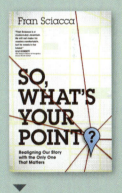

Some content taken from *SO, WHAT'S YOUR POINT?* by Fran Sciacca.

Copyright © 2015. Used by permission of NavPress. All rights reserved.

5.
COMMITMENT

If, as the findings show, apathy is the primary obstacle to healthy discipleship, the solution is to make discipleship a priority. In exemplar churches, discipleship is not a program or even a "ministry"; it is part of the church's core identity. There is vision among the senior leadership for what healthy discipleship should look like, and this vision appears to ripple out to the entire Body. Two-thirds of exemplar church leaders say discipleship is among the top three priorities for their senior pastor; the other one-third considers it *the* top priority.

Exemplar interviews make it clear that these leaders have thought deeply about discipleship, have a clear perspective on it and maintain a passion for it. They believe making and growing disciples is Jesus' singular commission to the Church, and they pursue it with intention and intensity.

Three-quarters of exemplar churches say that the vision or endorsement of senior leadership and a clearly articulated plan or approach to discipleship are both critical to their efforts. Additionally, their church's prioritization of overall spiritual development reflects a clear commitment to discipleship—not just at the leadership level, but throughout the congregation.

IN EXEMPLAR CHURCHES, DISCIPLESHIP IS NOT A PROGRAM OR EVEN A "MINISTRY"; IT IS PART OF THE CHURCH'S CORE IDENTITY.

Three-quarters or more of exemplar leaders say the following factors are critical to their discipleship efforts:

- Senior leaders modeling discipleship
- Church-wide commitment to Scripture
- Well-trained lay leaders

Pastors agree in principle that the engagement of senior leadership in discipleship is important. Among the broader population of church leaders, 61 percent say it is among their church's top three priorities and 26 percent consider it their number-one priority. Eight percent say it is not a top-three priority and 4 percent say "discipleship is not something they are actively addressing at this time." Although most leaders believe they are prioritizing discipleship, participation rates in most churches do not reflect this pastoral emphasis. Leader assessments of discipleship's priority thus appear to be overly optimistic.

One reason for skepticism about the priority placed on discipleship by many churches is the level of senior-pastor involvement in discipleship: Half of church leaders say the senior pastor has primary responsibility for discipleship. Only 8 percent have a discipleship pastor to whom the responsibility falls. The balance of responsibility for active discipleship falls on elders and deacons, Sunday school teachers, small group leaders and other lay leaders.

As mentioned above, exemplar leaders say that having a clearly articulated plan is a key factor in a thriving discipleship program—and this is an area where many church leaders see room for improvement. When asked what they would like to see improved in their discipleship programs, a clear plan is selected by a plurality of senior pastors (28%) and discipleship leaders (23%). Increased interest is second, with 16 percent of church leaders mentioning this factor.

HALF OF CHURCH LEADERS SAY THE SENIOR PASTOR HAS PRIMARY RESPONSIBILITY FOR DISCIPLESHIP.

DESIRED CHANGES IN HOW THE CHURCH DISCIPLES

Q: If your church could do one thing differently when it comes to how it disciples, what would you want to change?

	All Church Leaders	Senior Pastors	Discipleship Leaders
Develop a more clearly articulated plan, or approach, to discipleship	27%	28%	23%
More interest in becoming a disciple	16	17	11
More well-trained lay leaders	10	11	8
More volunteers	7	7	8
Senior leadership modeling discipleship better	5	4	8
More programs	3	3	5
Undertake regular assessments of progress	2	2	2
Senior leadership endorsement	1	2	1
More paid staff	1	1	2
More money to spend on purchasing resources	1	1	1
Other	22	20	29
Not sure	4	4	2

COMMITMENT

6.
ASSESSMENT

The gap between church leaders' self-assessment of how they prioritize discipleship and their churches' rates of participation in discipleship activities raises a question: *How are churches assessing the success of their discipleship efforts?*

The research shows that exemplar churches track discipleship much more closely and consistently than other churches. They are intentional about assessing progress. This is accomplished in part by observing "soft" measures: fruits of the Spirit among members, passion for sharing faith, individuals making God-honoring life decisions. Participation and leadership are the most common objective indicators: the number of people engaged in small groups or Bible studies, the number of new leaders, and the number of individuals serving inside and outside the church. Approximately half of exemplar churches also use surveys or self-assessments.

In order to ensure healthy growth, exemplars invest significantly in leadership development. Many also say their definition of discipleship has expanded from individual growth in Christ to include "making disciples." This is because real, healthy disciples should naturally produce more disciples. More than half refer to making disciples as an important component of discipleship. Many have leadership classes or other training regimens specifically for discipleship leaders. As one exemplar leader wrote: "This is the ultimate determination of success for the process. Without multiplication, we've simply had another Bible study benefitting

MANY EXEMPLARS SAY THEIR DEFINITION OF DISCIPLESHIP HAS EXPANDED FROM INDIVIDUAL GROWTH IN CHRIST TO INCLUDE "MAKING DISCIPLES." THIS IS BECAUSE REAL, HEALTHY DISCIPLES SHOULD NATURALLY PRODUCE MORE DISCIPLES.

the local body. With multiplication, the impact will spread outside the walls of our church to the ends of the earth."

Compared with exemplars, when senior pastors and discipleship leaders are asked how their church tracks and assesses discipleship effectiveness, responses indicate that effectiveness is *not* tracked, or done so only informally. Tracking methods mentioned by church leaders include simple metrics such as service attendance, participation in classes (including discipleship classes, Bible studies, Sunday school and small groups) and overall numbers of members and baptisms. Other assessment metrics mentioned are observational or anecdotal, such as pastoral conversations with church members, observations by discipleship group leaders and discussions among staff of perceived growth, and observed individual behavior such as increased participation in church leadership and activities, becoming more Christ-like and being trained or equipped to become a discipler.

When asked how they measure discipleship effectiveness, some leaders describe the process of discipleship and the programs they have in place, rather than how they evaluate results. Less than 1 percent of pastors report using an actual survey or other evaluation instrument.

Accordingly, equipping churches to develop a plan and measure its results could produce significant progress in the area of discipleship.

FOUR REFLECTIONS ON THE STATE OF DISCIPLESHIP

BY PRESTON SPRINKLE

The statistics from Barna's study reveal several interesting reflections on the state of discipleship in the church.

First, almost everyone recognizes that the Church as a whole is not doing a good job making disciples and that something needs to change. There are disagreements, however, about what needs to change. Some aspects are more agreeable than others. Many leaders seem to recognize that the program model isn't (and probably never really was) working. Our 8-week, 12-week or 40-week programs where one speaker teaches a large group of "disciples" doesn't get to the heart of what it takes to make disciples. Plus, putting a terminal date on the program (12 weeks, 40 weeks, etc.) assumes a wrong view of discipleship. *Discipleship is for life*.

Most leaders rightly emphasize that authentic relationships in small group settings are the best avenues for discipleship. Even better are models where there is more of a "shared life," where the discipler and disciple do more than just meet once a week for coffee. I'm not sure what this looks like practically, but in my forthcoming book I plan on talking about some examples where this is actually happening.

Also, I think the model where the older, mature, more holy "discipler" teaches the younger, less mature "disciple," needs to be challenged (as Greg Ogden and Jonathan Dodson have done in their writing). I think we need more authenticity and vulnerability from the "leader," who is really a leader among equals and just as much a broken disciple as those whom he's discipling.

Second, the study reveals some disagreement about what discipleship is and how it's defined. Most leaders, though, say it has to do with "becoming more like Christ," and this is true, I believe.

I think more attention needs to be given to articulating what it means to "be like Christ." It sometimes feels like we've created a 21st-century American suburban Jesus who is most concerned with personal morality. But the Middle Eastern peasant who was crucified for political and religious treason is who we're seeking to be like. Jesus hung out with people most Christians try to avoid. He lived so close to unholy people that he developed a reputation of being a drunk and a glutton. He loved his enemies and challenged the religious status quo every chance he got. All that to say, we need to de-cliché our language; we need to unpack what it means to actually become like the Jesus who is revealed to us in the Gospels.

Third, most Christians express a desire to grow and yet don't appear to flesh out this desire. Busyness and apathy are among the reasons they aren't engaged in a discipling activity (Bible study, small group, Sunday school, etc.).

I have three thoughts or questions about this. 1) Should we measure discipleship in terms of such church activities? Discipleship is more of an identity than an activity; understanding and believing who we are shapes what we do. Discipleship must begin with a firm understanding and belief in our identity as co-crucified sons and daughters of God. 2) The types of discipleship activities should also be re-examined. Sunday schools and Bible studies appear to be a thing of the past—for good or for ill (probably both). Many (especially younger) Christians are hungering for more real-life, tangible and authentic activities that are centered on *doing* rather than *learning*. These may include community service projects or ministries that address local and global injustices (sex trafficking, poverty relief, racial reconciliation, etc.). These types of activities shouldn't replace, but complement the traditional learning-based activities. Discipleship is both about *learning* and *doing*, which are rooted in *being*. 3) Christians—all people, really—gravitate toward and make time for the things they desire and value. I wonder if the content of our discipleship (the teaching/learning aspects) should be more holistic. One of the biggest complaints among Millennials is that they aren't told how the gospel relates to everyday interests: vocation, politics, music, art, science and so on. Discipleship shouldn't just focus on personal morality. It must cultivate and form an entire Christian worldview.

Fourth, we need to consider the role of grace or the gospel in discipleship. This may be a hard thing to assess and measure in research, but I would be curious to find out if a lame view of grace has contributed to the lack of desire for discipleship. Anecdotally, I see this as a major hindrance

> Discipleship must cultivate and form an entire Christian worldview.

all the time. Christians are defeated by performance-driven approaches to the faith; the thought of pursuing discipleship feels like one more spiritual activity that they are going to fail.

It seems like much of the emphasis is on our pursuit of God, but there's little emphasis on God's pursuit of us. Since discipleship is primarily an identity, then our identity as loved and forgiven objects of God's scandalous delight must be foundational to our pursuit of God. I just wonder if fear—the fear of man, fear of failure, fear of being known and the fear that God could never use someone as messed up as me—is at least part of the reason why some people don't begin or persevere in discipling relationships.

PRESTON SPRINKLE, PH.D. serves as Vice President for Eternity Bible College's Boise extension and has authored several books, including the *New York Times* bestselling *Erasing Hell* (with Francis Chan). He has been featured on dozens of radio shows across the country, frequently writes for *RELEVANT* magazine, and hosts a daily radio program and podcast, *What Does the Bible Really Say?* Preston lives in Boise, Idaho, with his wife and four kids.

7.
RESOURCES

What role do resources play in addressing a church's need to make discipleship a personal and corporate priority? What do pastors, leaders and disciples think of the resources currently available?

Most churches value discipleship materials enough to account for them in their budgets. On average, churches allocate 21 percent of their budget to discipleship; this may include leadership time leveraged against discipleship activities and administration, as well as allocation for resources. This is fairly consistent across different types of churches and leaders.

There is solid demand for discipleship materials: Six in 10 church leaders believe it is "very valuable" for someone to be involved in a systematic curriculum or program of discipleship (59%), and another one-third says it is "somewhat valuable" (34%). The preference for a structured curriculum is higher in majority black churches (80% say curriculum is "very valuable") than in white (56%).

Few church leaders—only one in five—suggest there is a need for more or better materials and resources for discipleship (21%); about as many say there are *too many* resources (19%). In contrast, about half of exemplar leaders express a need for new and more resources. However, many exemplars say they prefer to write their own curriculum tailored to their congregation, and that there is "nothing better than the Book."

NAVIGATORS MATERIALS ENJOY A VERY GOOD REPUTATION AMONG THOSE WHO HAVE USED THEM.

While Navigators is not the first organization church leaders or Christian adults think of in terms of discipleship resources, Navigators materials enjoy a very good reputation among those who have used them. One-quarter of leaders say their church has used a Navigators discipleship curriculum at some point (27%), and 17 percent of Christians report having used a Navigators program.

AWARENESS OF ORGANIZATIONS

Church leaders list a broad range of authors and ministries they most associate with discipleship. Navigators and LifeWay top the list, with approximately 6 percent mentioning these unaided. Other top responses include Francis Chan, Rick Warren/Saddleback Church, Andy Stanley, David Platt, Max Lucado, John Macarthur/*Grace to You* and Dallas Willard.

Non-Navigators discipleship resources mentioned include materials from Bible Study Fellowship, Cru/Campus Crusade and Daily Bread. Specific books and authors mentioned include:

- Mark Dever, *9 Marks of a Healthy Church*

- Robert Coleman, *Master Plan of Evangelism*

- Jim Putman, *Real-Life Discipleship*

- Colin Marshal, *The Trellis and the Vine*

- Francis Chan, *Multiply*

Christian adults think of very few ministries, pastors or authors; most refer to general resources: "my church" or "the Bible." Mentioned unaided by more than one percent are Billy Graham, Joyce Meyer, Charles Stanley and Joel Osteen.

Among a list of 10 discipleship organizations, the most commonly recognized is Promise Keepers, with nearly universal recognition among church leaders (92%) and 39 percent of Christian adults familiar with the name. FCA (Fellowship of Christian Athletes), Cru (formerly Campus Crusade) and InterVarsity are familiar to most church leaders and a handful of Christians. Seven in 10 church leaders (72%) and one in seven Christians (15%) are familiar with The Navigators. The remaining five organizations are familiar to fewer than half of all church leaders and only a few Christian adults.

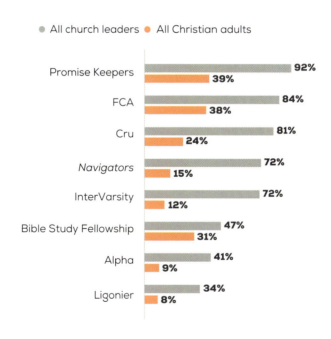

FAMILIARITY WITH DISCIPLESHIP ORGANIZATIONS

% among Christian adults and church leaders

● All church leaders ● All Christian adults

Organization	All church leaders	All Christian adults
Promise Keepers	92%	39%
FCA	84%	38%
Cru	81%	24%
Navigators	72%	15%
InterVarsity	72%	12%
Bible Study Fellowship	47%	31%
Alpha	41%	9%
Ligonier	34%	8%

IMPRESSIONS OF ORGANIZATIONS

Among Christian adults familiar with each organization, impressions are most positive for Bible Study Fellowship (53% "very positive") and FCA (46%). Church leaders have relatively similar perceptions of organizations mentioned, with Navigators near the top in favorable impressions.

IMPRESSIONS OF DISCIPLESHIP ORGANIZATIONS

Q: What is your impression of this organization?
% very positive (among those familiar with organization)

	All Church Leaders	Senior Pastors	Discipleship Leaders	All Christians
Renovare	39%	38%	NA	NA
Fellowship of Christian Athletes	35	35	31	46
Navigators	35	33	42	35
Bible Study Fellowship	33	31	42	53
Cru (formerly Campus Crusade)	31	30	35	37
Ligonier Ministries	32	29	NA	34
Alpha	29	28	NA	25
InterVarsity	28	27	32	35
Promise Keepers	24	23	27	39
Scripture Union	17	19	NA	43

OWNING THE DISCIPLESHIP SPACE

Among Christian adults who have used Navigators resources, about half consider the two most commonly used, the *Life Change Series* and *Studies in Christian Living*, "very helpful." Other Navigators resources used receive similar reviews from Christians.

About three in 10 church leaders consider each of the Navigators resources "very helpful" and just over half say they are "somewhat helpful." *Topical Memory System* is considered most helpful among leaders who have used the program (35% very helpful).

USE OF NAVIGATORS PROGRAMS

Q: Has your church ever used any of the following discipleship resources? (church leaders)

Q: Have you ever used any of the following discipleship resources? (adults whose spiritual growth is at least somewhat important)

	All Church Leaders	Senior Pastors	Discipleship Leaders	All Christians	Practicing Christians	Non-practicing Christians
Life Change Series	11%	12%	9%	6%	7%	3%
Studies in Christian Living	10	8	15	9	11	6
Design for Discipleship	9	9	10	4	5	2
Topical Memory System	6	7	5	4	5	2
The 2:7 Series	7	6	9	3	3	2
Ways of the Alongsider	1	1	0	1	1	1
None of these	73	73	71	83	81	88

HELPFULNESS OF NAVIGATORS PROGRAMS

Q: How helpful was [program]?
(% "very helpful" among those who had used each program)

	Senior Pastors	Discipleship Leaders
Topical Memory System	35%	56%
The 2:7 Series	31	NA
Life Change Series	31	46
Design for Discipleship	29	55
Studies in Christian Living	20	50
Ways of the Alongsider	NA	NA

NA: not shown due to limited sample size.

Despite relatively healthy impressions of Navigators among Christians, there is a significant gap when it comes to associating Navigators with discipleship. Only 8 percent of Christian adults say Navigators is the best in this area. They are more likely to say Bible Study Fellowship (31%) or Promise Keepers (25%) are closely associated in their minds with discipleship.

However, Navigators comes out on top among church leaders, with one-quarter of pastors (26%) and discipleship leaders (27%) selecting this organization as "best at enabling discipleship." Thus, Navigators enjoys a healthy positioning with leaders, but has room to grow its reputation among the broader Christian audience.

BEST DISCIPLESHIP ORGANIZATIONS

Q: Which one or two organizations would you say are best at enabling discipleship?
(among those familiar with at least two organizations)

	All Church Leaders	Senior Pastors	Discipleship Leaders	All Christians	Practicing Christians	Non-practicing Christians
Navigators	26%	26%	27%	8%	10%	5%
Cru (formerly Campus Crusade)	20	19	23	15	17	8
Fellowship of Christian Athletes	17	17	18	22	22	23
Promise Keepers	15	16	14	25	28	18
InterVarsity	14	13	18	5	6	2
Alpha	12	11	15	3	3	4
Bible Study Fellowship	11	11	13	31	28	39
Renovare	6	6	5	1	1	1
Ligonier Ministries	5	5	6	3	3	3
Scripture Union	1	2	0	2	2	4
Other	5	6	3	NA	NA	NA
None of these	9	9	9	10	8	14
Not sure	12	14	5	4	4	5

NA: Option not presented in adult survey.

8.
MILLENNIALS

This study reveals some differences in the way Millennials think about and practice discipleship compared with older generations. For the most part these differences are minor; however, data show a shift by generation that suggests a trend that may continue over time.

Looking at definitions for discipleship reveals its goals to some degree. Millennials' choice of terminology for discipleship is largely the same as other generations except for "becoming more Christ-like": Boomers are most likely to select this label at 46 percent, followed by 41 percent of Gen-Xers and only 38 percent of Millennials. Nevertheless, this is still the most commonly chosen name for spiritual growth among young adults.

"Knowing Christ more deeply" is more commonly chosen by Millennials (63%) as a key goal of spiritual growth, compared with Gen-Xers and Boomers (56% each). Millennials are less likely to say "learning to live a more consistent Christian life" is a key goal (53%, vs. 59% of Gen-Xers, 62% of Boomers and 66% of Elders). This indicates that the idea of behavior-focused sanctification is waning over generations, replaced for the most part by a relational measure of spiritual health—confirming the aptness of exemplar churches' shift in this direction.

Regarding relationships, Millennials have a similar perception to older adults of how their faith could and should impact those around them. The exception is that they, and Gen-Xers, are more likely to believe their faith has an impact on relatives (41% each, vs. 33% of Boomers and 36% of Elders), rather than being a private affair.

> "Programs are being replaced by relationships. This Millennial generation wants the latter. We need to respond in kind, while holding fast to the biblical model outlined and fulfilled in Jesus."
>
> Christian educator

Younger generations are slightly less concerned in general about spiritual growth. Fifty-eight percent of Millennials consider it "very important" to see spiritual progress in their life, compared with 61 percent of Gen-Xers and Boomers and 67 percent of Elders. Among the reasons they desire spiritual progress in their lives, Millennials are more likely than older generations to cite a need for healing. Thirty-six percent say "I have been through a lot, and growing spiritually will help me," compared with 33 percent of Gen-Xers, 30 percent of Boomers and 27 percent of Elders. Millennials also are less likely than other generations to say "I think it is important to be improving or growing in general."

Young adults are far more likely to consider the general "busyness of life" a major obstacle to their spiritual growth. Among those who consider spiritual growth very or somewhat important, 38 percent of Millennials say busyness is a major obstacle, compared with 27 percent of Gen-Xers, 17 percent of Boomers and 11 percent of Elders. The realities of life stages suggest that Gen-Xers should feel most overwhelmed by the demands of life (career, children, home ownership, etc.); Millennials' assertion that busyness is a significant barrier may be due to broader factors such as a pervasive sense of bombardment by technology and social media.

Not surprisingly, Millennials are the most likely to currently use digital media—specifically, podcasts—for the purpose of spiritual growth. One-quarter of those who believe spiritual growth is very or somewhat important say they listen to podcasts about the Bible or related topics at least monthly (24%). This is in contrast to 15 percent of Gen-Xers and 10 percent of Boomers who listen to podcasts.

The relationships that seem to be most influential in Millennials' spiritual growth are somewhat distinct from other generations. Not surprisingly, more of them say "friends" have been "very helpful" to their spiritual growth (47%, vs. 33% of Gen-Xers and 39% among Boomers who say spiritual growth is important). In addition, 39 percent of spiritually growing Millennials say a "Christian community other than a church" has been "very helpful" to their spiritual growth, compared with 31 percent among Gen-Xers, 30 percent of Boomers and 25 percent of Elders. Online social networks are considered "very helpful" by 14 percent of

> "On the surface, there is a hunger, an openness, a willingness to be transformed in order to serve. That is a good thing. And on the part of many, a willingness to take personal ownership over their own growth. There is, however, a sense of entitlement/urgency, which wants what they want NOW without having to put in the long, hard, and sometimes frustrating work of using the classical disciplines to put ourselves in a place where Christ can transform us from the inside out."
>
> Christian educator

Millennials who consider spiritual growth at least somewhat important, compared with 11 percent of Gen-Xers and 9 percent of Boomers among the same segment.

Despite these propensities for social interaction, Millennials are more likely than other generations to prefer one-on-one or solitary discipleship structures. Forty percent of Millennials who consider spiritual growth very or somewhat important prefer on-their-own discipleship, compared with 36 percent among Gen-Xers and 32 percent of Elders (and 39 percent of Boomers, who are more like Millennials in this respect).

Twenty-one percent of Millennials who consider spiritual growth important prefer one-on-one mentoring models, compared with 14 percent among Gen-Xers and 16 percent of Boomers and Elders. Slightly more Millennials than other generations are currently in a one-on-one discipleship relationship. Twenty-eight percent of Millennials who consider spiritual growth important are currently being discipled, contrasted with 25 percent of Gen-Xers and 22 percent of Boomers.

In summary, young adults tend to think of spiritual growth as a deepening relationship with God rather than as changed outward behavior. They value relationships and friendships in the context of spiritual growth. Millennials are more likely to feel overwhelmed or bombarded, which hinders their involvement in structured discipleship. However, past struggles and a need for healing may drive their desire for spiritual growth more than other generations.

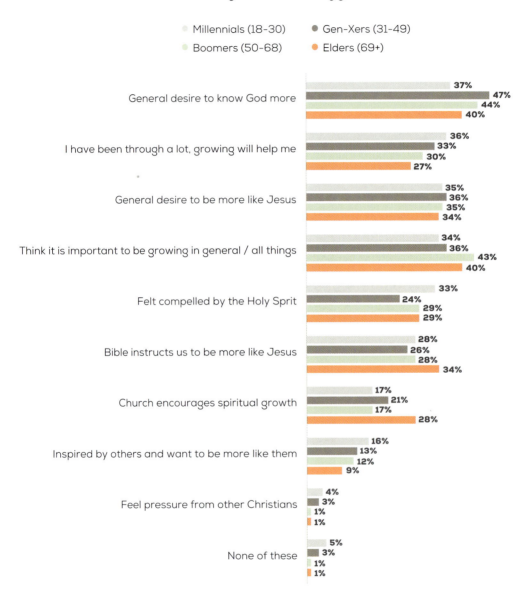

BARNA GROUP ON MILLENNIALS

Over the past decade, Barna has interviewed nearly 30,000 Millennials in more than 200 studies. These data validate findings in The Navigators' State of Discipleship study that Millennials desire meaningful relationships, often feel overwhelmed and struggle to make connections between faith and the rest of their lives.

Millennials' technology habits have an impact on their social and emotional well-being. One example: 49 percent of adults 18 to 30 years old acknowledge that their personal electronics separate them from other people, compared with 35 percent of all adults.

The effects run deeper than mere distraction. In 2001, about one in eight Americans self-identified as lonely (12%). By 2012, that number had *doubled*—a paradoxical reality in the social-media age. While loneliness among Americans has risen, the desire to find one's place among a few good friends has likewise increased from 31 percent a decade ago to 37 percent today. Leading this charge toward finding friendship are Millennials at 47 percent.

Barna research has uncovered significant differences between twentysomethings who have remained active in their faith after high school and twentysomethings who have dropped out of church. For instance, those who stay are *twice as likely* to have had a close personal friendship with an adult in their church (59%, compared to 31% among those who are no longer active). The same pattern is evident when it comes to intentional relationships such as mentoring; nearly three in 10 active Millennials had an adult mentor at the church other than their pastor (28%), compared to the just one in 10 dropouts who report the same (11%).

In addition to loneliness and a lack of meaningful relationships, 35 percent of Americans said in 2012 that they were "stressed out"; just 21 percent felt this way in 2001. Millennials especially feel this sense of

> Millennials often feel overwhelmed and struggle to make connections between faith and the rest of their lives.

being overwhelmed by life: 25 percent say they felt physically or mentally overwhelmed *five or more times* in the previous month, compared with 21 percent of all adults.

Having grown up with ubiquitous information technology, they often feel a sense of bombardment and are compelled to be "always on." Forty-two percent of Millennials, compared with 36 percent of all adults, say they usually stop what they're doing to check their phone when a text messages comes in; 56 percent, versus 40 percent of all adults, check their phone first thing in the morning; and 54 percent of Millennials, compared with 33 percent of all adults, check their phone right before going to bed.

Nearly four out of 10 young adults with a Christian background say they desire to follow Jesus in a way that connects with the world they live in (38%). Thanks to technology, information is pervasive; Millennials have greater access to knowledge than any generation in history. What they desire is *wisdom*—spiritual understanding that allows them to put knowledge into practice. They want to know how to interact with today's culture in a way that is consistent with their beliefs.

One of the most important areas where faith must connect to their lives is their work; career is paramount for Millennials. Thirty-seven percent expect to make an impact through their work within the first five years, and another 28 percent expect to do so in six or more years. Churches can deepen their connection with Millennials by focusing on vocational *calling*, outside of traditional church-based ministry. Millennials who have remained active in their faith (45%) are three times more likely than church dropouts (17%) to say they learned to view their gifts and passions as part of God's calling. They are also four times more likely to have learned "how the Bible applies to my field or career interests" (29% vs. 7% of dropouts).

> Churches can deepen their connection with Millennials by focusing on vocational *calling*, outside of traditional church-based ministry.

IMPLICATIONS & RECOMMENDATIONS

Many findings from the State of Discipleship study suggest that churches need the approach to discipleship that The Navigators has historically embraced and imparted: relational, intentional, organic (rather than systematized) and spiritually transformative. This presents a great opportunity for Navigators to be a strong voice and much-needed leader in these changing times by emphasizing what the organization already knows and does best.

RELATIONAL

Millennials (and older adults, too) isolated by personal technology crave real-life, face-to-face relationships with individuals and small groups. The younger generation also desires wisdom—not just knowledge—to navigate changing times and culture. One-on-one mentoring is the ideal setting to deliver this type of guidance, fostering deep relationship that leads to transformation and serves as an anchor for continuing engagement with the Church. In a culture of isolation, discipleship relationships are an open door for spiritual transformation.

How are these one-on-one and small-group relationships established? Among the broader Christian population, the catalyst for existing

> **IN A CULTURE OF ISOLATION, DISCIPLESHIP RELATIONSHIPS ARE AN OPEN DOOR FOR SPIRITUAL TRANSFORMATION.**

one-on-one mentoring relationships is unclear and variable, suggesting there may be many ways leaders can spawn such relationships: through church, work, community-based or volunteer activities, or even social media. Millennials indicate a desire to better integrate their faith into their lives and respond positively to notions of "whole-life discipleship." This desire may be an area for further testing and development, to identify best practices for catalyzing discipleship relationships based on their needs.

INTENTIONAL

Our time-starved, always-on culture means the cost of discipleship, in time and attention, feels higher than ever to both leaders and participants. Data from this research show a lack of initiative toward investing in personal spiritual growth, even when Christians express a desire to grow. What is necessary, then, for Christians to make the investment of time necessary for real spiritual growth? *Intentionality* and *accountability*.

Exemplars foster intentionality by creating a church-wide culture of discipleship. Senior leaders support the vision, model transformative disciplines and shape their church around the goal of spiritual transformation. Discipleship is a top priority, and they are intentional about keeping it that way. They communicate this intentionality in word and by example to their flock.

Our culture's propensity for "busyness" also coincides with the need for whole-life discipleship—to meet people where they live, work and play. Rather than organizing all activities at the church, effective discipleship is intentionally integrated physically and conceptually into the workplace, community, social media and more. If people are scattered, then perhaps churches must be as well.

Accountability is essential for busy, scattered people to make the time to invest in their spiritual growth. Small groups and one-on-one relationships, in particular, provide excellent structure for accountability and encourage commitment to make time for discipleship.

ORGANIC

Gone are the days when one-size-fits-all, systematic models of discipleship were effective. Christians, and especially young adults, desire conversation and relationship, not imparting of knowledge, which require more organic, customized approaches. Exemplar churches have embraced this shift and say they create their own models and their own materials to fit the unique needs of their members.

These shifts present an opportunity for Navigators to create modular, customizable tools and training to guide discussions of life application in discipleship contexts. Navigators should continue to equip church leaders to better understand their members' needs and to employ tailored approaches that reach them where they are. This—more than content—is what leaders need for an organic, relevant approach to discipleship.

TRANSFORMATIVE

Church leaders who embrace a culture of discipleship describe a shift away from "head knowledge" toward life transformation. Further, leaders and Christians alike prefer the term "becoming more Christ-like." Both are great news for the future of the Church, as this phrase aligns with the ultimate goal of spiritual growth. It is more specific and evocative than "discipleship," which is vague and not as easily defined.

On many measures, Navigators alumni are more committed to spiritual growth even than church leaders, a testament to the coaching they have received from the organization. Alumni report excellent spiritual health and commitment to their own growth, and to the growth of people around them through mentoring and evangelism.

Given its track record, The Navigators is primed to be a chief advocate for relational, intentional, organic spiritual transformation. The organization's history and expertise with these concepts puts it in a key position to equip and provide resources to church leaders who wonder how to create transformative discipleship programs. Some work will be necessary, however, to refresh the presentation of these concepts and to ensure they are communicated and delivered in a way that is relevant to today's younger generation. Navigators is poised to equip the next generation to become more Christ-like and to pass faith on to the generation after them: *to know Christ and make Him known.*

THE NAVIGATORS IS PRIMED TO BE A CHIEF ADVOCATE FOR RELATIONAL, INTENTIONAL, ORGANIC SPIRITUAL TRANSFORMATION.

APPENDICES

A.
DATA TABLES

DEFINITIONS

Denominational Segments

- **MAINLINE:** includes American Baptist Churches, Episcopal, Evangelical Lutheran Church of America, United Church of Christ, United Methodist Church and Presbyterian Church, USA
- **NON-MAINLINE:** includes Protestant churches not included in mainline denominations
- **OTHER CHRISTIANS:** self-identified Christians who do not identify as attending a Mainline or Non-mainline church as described above

Leader Segments

- **SENIOR PASTORS:** church leaders who are the senior leader of their congregation
- **DISCIPLESHIP LEADERS:** church leaders whose ministry specifically focuses on discipleship
- **ALL CHURCH LEADERS:** senior pastors and discipleship leaders combined

Faith Segments

- **SELF-IDENTIFIED CHRISTIANS:** those who select "Christian" when asked to identify their religion; also sometimes called "all Christians"
- **PRACTICING CHRISTIANS:** self-identified Christians who have attended a church service, other than for a special occasion such as a wedding or holiday, at least once during the past month and who say their faith is very important in their life today
- **NON-PRACTICING CHRISTIANS:** self-identified Christians who do not qualify as "practicing" under the criteria above
- **NAVIGATORS ALUMNI:** respondents who have participated in a Navigators discipleship program

1. DEFINING DISCIPLESHIP

Table 1.1
TERMS USED TO DESCRIBE SPIRITUAL GROWTH

Q: Would you use any of these words to describe the process of spiritual growth?
(Two answers allowed)

	All Church Leaders	Senior Pastors	Discipleship Leaders	All Christians	Practicing Christians	Non-practicing Christians	Navigators Alumni
Becoming more Christ-like	51%	51%	49%	43%	54%	25%	55%
Discipleship	46	45	46	17	23	8	49
Sanctification	26	25	28	9	11	5	41
Spiritual growth	21	20	22	31	30	33	18
Spiritual formation	17	18	16	5	5	5	10
Spiritual journey	16	17	15	28	24	33	2
Spiritual maturation	14	14	14	16	15	17	18
None of these	1	1	1	8	3	18	0
Not sure	0	0	1	1	0	1	0

Table 1.2
RELEVANCE OF "DISCIPLESHIP" WHEN DESCRIBING SPIRITUAL GROWTH

	All Christians	Practicing Christians	Non-practicing Christians	Navigators Alumni
Q: Some Christians use the term "discipleship" to describe a process of spiritual growth. How relevant is the term "discipleship" to you, when you think of the process of spiritual growth? *(% among those who did not choose "discipleship" as preferred term)*				
Very relevant	28%	41%	10%	84%
Somewhat relevant	37	40	33	12
Not too relevant	19	12	28	4
Not at all relevant	16	7	28	0
Not sure	1	0	1	0

Table 1.3
AGREEMENT ON "DISCIPLESHIP" TO DESCRIBE SPIRITUAL GROWTH PROCESS

	All Church Leaders	Senior Pastors	Discipleship Leaders
Q: For the purposes of this survey, we are going to use the word "discipleship." This may or may not be exactly what you have in mind when you think of "[term selected]". Would you consider "discipleship" and "[term selected]" the same, similar, or different? *(% who did not select "discipleship")*			
The same	47%	45%	53%
Similar	43	45	39
Different	10	9	9
Not sure	0	1	0

Table 1.4
GOAL OF DISCIPLESHIP

Q: People often have different ways of defining the goal of discipleship. For each of the following please tell me if each term is one you'd use to describe the primary goal or goals of discipleship.

	All Church Leaders	Senior Pastors	Discipleship Leaders	All Christians	Practicing Christians	Non-practicing Christians	Navigators Alumni
Being transformed to become more like Jesus	89%	87%	94%	45%	53%	32%	84%
Growing in spiritual maturity	83	79	94	55	61	46	57
Knowing Christ more deeply	83	78	95	58	65	47	67
Becoming more obedient to God	77	73	88	55	63	42	39
Learning to live a more consistent Christian life	77	72	90	60	66	50	45
Mentoring and being mentored in the area of Christian maturity	77	71	92	50	59	35	74
Learning to trust in God more	75	71	86	59	63	51	39
Deepening one's faith through education and fellowship	72	67	87	56	62	46	35
Winning new believers to become followers of Jesus Christ	59	56	69	46	55	31	33
Don't know / Never thought about it	0	0	0	7	2	15	0

Table 1.5
DEFINITIONS OF DISCIPLESHIP: CHURCH LEADERS

Q: When you think about the idea of discipleship, which one of the following comes closest to how you define it?
(online only; n = 290)

	All Church Leaders
Discipleship is the process where a person purposely joins God to increasingly follow and live like Jesus, through the Scriptures, the Holy Spirit, and the input of others.	26%
Discipleship is the process of learning to follow Jesus Christ as Savior and Lord, seeking to observe all that Jesus commanded, by the power of the Holy Spirit and to the glory of God the Father.	24
Discipleship is the process of transformation that changes us to be increasingly more like Christ through the Word, the Spirit, and circumstance.	20
Discipleship is a lifelong process and journey rooted in a relationship with Jesus.	14
Discipleship is becoming more and more like Jesus and letting Him live His life more and more in me.	8
Discipleship is about connecting with someone who will help you connect with God for the purpose of fulfilling your God-given destiny.	5
Other / none of these	3

Table 1.6
DEFINITIONS OF DISCIPLESHIP: CHRISTIAN ADULTS

Q: The following are some definitions that some people might use to describe "discipleship." Please rank order these phrases in order of which comes closest to how you think about discipleship, where the top (#1) is closest and the bottom (#6) is furthest from how you would describe discipleship.

(mean rank; online survey only; n = 1,300)

	All Christian Adults	Navigators Alumni
Discipleship is a lifelong process and journey rooted in a relationship with Jesus.	2.9	3.9
Discipleship is the process of learning to follow Jesus Christ as Savior and Lord, seeking to observe all that Jesus commanded, by the power of the Holy Spirit and to the glory of God the Father.	3.0	2.7
Discipleship is the process of transformation that changes us to be increasingly more like Christ through the Word, the Spirit, and circumstance.	3.4	3.1
Discipleship is the process where a person purposely joins God to increasingly follow and live like Jesus, through the scriptures, the Holy Spirit, and the input of others.	3.6	3.0
Discipleship is becoming more and more like Jesus and letting Him live His life more and more in me.	3.6	3.6
Discipleship is about connecting with someone who will help you connect with God for the purpose of fulfilling your God-given destiny.	4.5	4.6

2. SPIRITUAL HEALTH

Table 2.1
PERCEPTIONS OF CHURCH'S EMPHASIS ON SPIRITUAL GROWTH

	All Christians	Practicing Christians	Non-practicing Christians
Q: Thinking about the church you attend most often, how much emphasis would you say that church places on growing in your spiritual life? *(% among those whose spiritual growth is at least somewhat important)*			
A lot	67%	73%	40%
Some	27	23	44
Not too much	4	3	9
None	1	0	7

Table 2.2
RATING TODAY'S CHURCHES ON DISCIPLESHIP

	All Church Leaders	Senior Pastors	Discipleship Leaders
Q: Overall, how well would you say today's churches are doing at discipling new and young believers?			
Very well	1%	1%	0%
Somewhat well	20	18	26
Not too	60	60	61
Not at all well	17	19	11
Not sure	3	3	2

Table 2.3
CURRENT INVOLVEMENT IN DISCIPLESHIP ACTIVITIES

Q: Which do you use or are you involved with now on a regular basis (at least monthly)?

(% among those who say spiritual growth is at least somewhat important)

	All Christians	Practicing Christians	Non-practicing Christians	Navigators Alumni
Regular prayer	71%	81%	53%	94%
Attending church worship services	64	84	27	94
Quiet time	56	61	45	95
Studying the Bible on your own	47	56	29	94
Listening to Christian music	43	53	24	71
Meditating on Scripture	33	43	15	88
Attending Sunday school or fellowship group	31	43	8	65
Studying the Bible with a group	23	33	6	69
A Bible study curriculum	21	28	7	49
Scripture memorization	20	26	11	59
Reading and discussing a Christian book with a group	18	25	5	47
Podcasts about the Bible or Christian life	14	17	8	34
Meeting with a spiritual mentor	14	17	7	53
A Christian student group in college	7	9	4	12
A Christian student group in high school	7	8	4	6
None of these	10	3	23	0

Table 2.4
PAST INVOLVEMENT IN DISCIPLESHIP ACTIVITIES

Q: Which of the following methods of discipleship have you ever used or been involved with?

(% among those who say spiritual growth is at least somewhat important)

	All Christians	Practicing Christians	Non-practicing Christians	Navigators Alumni
Attending church worship services	49%	46%	54%	71%
Attending Sunday school or fellowship group	48	47	50	67
Studying the Bible on your own	46	49	40	74
Studying the Bible with a group	44	48	36	74
Regular prayer	44	45	41	67
Listening to Christian music	41	44	34	71
Quiet time	38	40	35	76
Scripture memorization	39	44	30	80
A Bible study curriculum	39	44	29	82
Reading and discussing a Christian book with a group	37	40	30	82
A Christian student group in high school	36	41	27	88
Meditating on Scripture	35	40	27	71
A Christian student group in college	32	38	20	84
Meeting with a spiritual mentor	32	35	27	94
Podcasts about the Bible or Christian life	24	28	17	59
None of these	10	7	14	0

Table 2.5
DISCIPLESHIP METHODS RECOMMENDED BY CHURCH

Q: Which of these methods of discipleship does your church recommend?
(% among those who say spiritual growth is at least somewhat important)

	All Christians	Practicing Christians	Non-practicing Christians
Attending church worship services	54%	60%	41%
Regular prayer	50	58	36
Studying the Bible on your own	50	58	34
Attending Sunday school or fellowship group	50	56	40
Studying the Bible with a group	50	56	39
A Bible study curriculum	46	49	39
Meditating on Scripture	45	52	33
Reading and discussing a Christian book with a group	38	42	29
Quiet time	35	40	24
Meeting with a spiritual mentor	35	37	31
Scripture memorization	33	35	29
A Christian student group in high school	31	34	26
A Christian student group in college	30	33	25
Listening to Christian music	27	30	22
Podcasts about the Bible or Christian life	26	26	27
None of these	15	8	28

Table 2.6
ESTIMATE OF PERCENT OF MEMBERS INVOLVED IN DISCIPLESHIP

Q: What percent of your church's members are currently involved in some sort of discipleship group, relationship or program?

	All Church Leaders	Senior Pastors	Discipleship Leaders
less than 15 percent	13%	15%	7%
15-29 percent	17	18	14
30-44 percent	22	21	25
45-59 percent	17	16	19
60-74 percent	16	15	19
75 percent or more	16	15	17
mean	44	42	48
median	40	40	50

Table 2.7
HOURS CHURCH LEADERS THINK CONGREGANTS SPEND ON SPIRITUAL GROWTH

	All Church Leaders	Senior Pastors	Discipleship Leaders
Q: How many hours per week would you estimate a typical member of your church devotes to personal spiritual growth?			
1 or less	13%	13%	15%
2-3	40	38	43
4-5	23	24	21
6 or more	23	25	21
mean	4.5	4.5	4.6
median	3.0	3.0	3.0

Table 2.8
SPIRITUAL PROGRESS IN THE PAST YEAR

	All Christians	Practicing Christians	Non-practicing Christians	Navigators Alumni
Q: If you think about "spiritual progress" as growing and changing to become a more spiritually mature version of yourself, what progress would you say you have seen in your spiritual life in the past year?				
A lot	33%	40%	20%	43%
Some	49	51	43	53
Not much	13	7	22	4
No progress	6	2	12	0
No longer have a Christian faith	0	0	1	0

Table 2.9
SATISFACTION WITH SPIRITUAL LIFE

	All Christians	Practicing Christians	Non-practicing Christians	Navigators Alumni
Q: Many people are very satisfied with their spiritual life, while others feel like they need to constantly improve in this area. Which of the following descriptions best describes how you think about your spiritual journey?				
You're happy with where you are in your spiritual life	38%	35%	44%	100%
You're almost to where you want to be in your spiritual life	36	39	30	0
You're very far from where you want to be in your spiritual life	25	25	25	0
Not sure	1	1	0	0

Table 2.10
IMPORTANCE OF SPIRITUAL PROGRESS

	All Christians	Practicing Christians	Non-practicing Christians	Navigators Alumni
Q: How important is it to you that you see progress in your spiritual life?				
Very	62	77%	37%	94%
Somewhat	28	20	42	6
Not too	7	2	15	0
Not at all	3	1	5	0

Table 2.11

REASONS TO PURSUE SPIRITUAL GROWTH

Q: There are a lot of different reasons people desire to grow spiritually. Out of the following list, please tell me which you consider the top two or three most important reasons that you want to grow spiritually.

	All Christians	Practicing Christians	Non-practicing Christians	Navigators Alumni
I have a general desire to know Jesus, or God, more	43%	46%	36%	78%
I think it is important to be improving or growing in general / in all things	39	33	51	6
I have a general desire to be more like Jesus	35	41	25	82
I have been through a lot, and growing spiritually will help me	31	26	41	2
The Bible instructs us to be more like Jesus	29	34	18	33
I feel compelled by the Holy Spirit	28	33	19	51
My church encourages spiritual growth	20	24	12	2
I am inspired by other people, and want to be more like them	13	12	15	16
I feel pressure from other Christians	2	1	3	0

Table 2.12
SHOULD SPIRITUAL LIFE BE PRIVATE OR PUBLIC?

Q: Some people see their spiritual life as entirely private; other people consider their personal spiritual life relevant to other people. Do you consider your personal spiritual life to be . . . (Multiple response)

(% among those who feel spiritual growth is at least somewhat important)

	All Christians	Practicing Christians	Non-practicing Christians	Navigators Alumni
Entirely private	41%	28%	60%	0%
Having an impact on relatives	37	46	24	76
Having an impact on friends	36	47	19	78
Having an impact on your community	33	44	15	84
Having an impact on society	29	38	15	78
Other	10	12	8	22

3. MODELS

Table 3.1
PREFERRED METHOD OF DISCIPLESHIP

	All Christians	Practicing Christians	Non-practicing Christians	Navigators Alumni
Q: Which of the following is your most preferred method for discipleship? *(% among those who feel spiritual growth is at least somewhat important)*				
On your own	37%	30%	53%	4%
With a group	25	29	17	49
One-on-one with another person	16	18	13	2
A mix of these	21	23	16	45

Table 3.2
INVOLVEMENT IN DISCIPLESHIP / PERSONAL MENTORING

	All Church Leaders	Senior Pastors	Discipleship Leaders	All Christians	Practicing Christians	Non-practicing Christians	Navigators Alumni
Discipleship Relationships							
Personally active in discipling members of your church / others	94%	94%	95%	19%	25%	9%	51%
Personally being discipled by someone else	62	59	72	23	29	12	43

Table 3.3
HOW DISCIPLESHIP CONNECTION WAS MADE

Q: How did this discipleship connection come about?
(% currently being discipled / mentored)

	All Christians	Practicing Christians	Non-practicing Christians	Navigators Alumni
This person invited you into a discipling relationship	27%	27%	32%	29%
You were paired with this person by a church or ministry	23	23	19	24
Did you ask this person to disciple you	20	23	9	48
Or something else	28	26	35	0

Table 3.4
HOW DISCIPLERS CONNECT WITH DISCIPLEES

Q: How did this discipleship connection come about?
(% currently discipling someone else)

	All Christians	Practicing Christians	Non-practicing Christians	Navigators Alumni
This person invited you into a discipling relationship	29	30	NA	32%
You asked this person	18	19	NA	40
You were paired with this person by a church or ministry	12	13	NA	12
Something else	41	38	NA	16

NA: Percentage among Non-practicing Christians are not shown due to limited sample size.

Table 3.5
VALUABLE RELATIONSHIPS IN SPIRITUAL JOURNEY

Q: How valuable have each of the following types of relationships been when it comes to your spiritual journey? (% very valuable)

(% spiritual growth is at least somewhat important)

	All Christians	Practicing Christians	Non-practicing Christians
Family members	63%	67%	52%
People at your church	51	62	26
A Bible study or small group	49	61	22
Friends	40	42	36
A mentor	33	38	24
A Christian community other than a church	31	36	21
Online social networks	10	9	12

Table 3.6
MOST EFFECTIVE APPROACHES TO SPIRITUAL GROWTH

	All Church Leaders	Senior Pastors	Discipleship Leaders
Q: Which ONE of these do you think is most effective in producing spiritual growth – whether or not your church currently recommends it?			
Small group study or discussion group	52%	51%	55%
One-on-one discipleship or mentoring	29	30	24
Individual study or disciplines	11	11	12
Large group study or discussion group	5	5	6
None of these	2	2	2

Table 3.7
APPROACHES TO SPIRITUAL GROWTH RECOMMENDED BY LEADERS

	All Church Leaders	Senior Pastors	Discipleship Leaders
Q: Which of the following approaches to spiritual growth does your church recommend to its members?			
Small group study or discussion group	90%	89%	93%
Individual study or disciplines	87	85	91
Large group study or discussion group	65	62	72
One-on-one discipleship or mentoring	61	58	69
None of these	0	1	0

Table 3.8
ESSENTIAL ELEMENTS FOR DISCIPLESHIP

Q: Which of these do you think are essential for discipleship?

	All Church Leaders	Senior Pastors	Discipleship Leaders
Time with God	94%	93%	98%
Prayer and meditation	95	93	98
Personal commitment to grow in Christ-likeness	94	92	99
Attending a local church	91	89	96
A deep love for God	90	88	95
An attitude of humility	85	81	94
Participating in a community / group with shared belief	83	80	93
Genuine, vulnerable relationships	79	75	87
Regular repentance of sins	77	73	88
A spiritual mentor or model	76	73	84
A systematized study of the Bible	65	64	67
In-depth education about the Bible	64	60	73
A comprehensive discipleship curriculum	44	40	54
None of these are essential	0	0	0
Not sure	0	0	0

Table 3.9
HELPFULNESS OF DISCIPLESHIP METHODS

Q: Which ones have been most helpful for your own spiritual journey?
(% among those who have used each)

	All Christian Adults	Navigators Alumni
Regular prayer	59%	57%
Attending church worship services	55	27
Quiet time	40	78
Studying the Bible on your own	38	63
Studying the Bible with a group	31	65
Meditating on Scripture	25	61
Meeting with a spiritual mentor	24	84
Attending Sunday school or fellowship group	22	18
Listening to Christian music	22	16
A Bible study curriculum	19	22
Reading and discussing a Christian book with a group	14	16
Scripture memorization	11	61
Podcasts about the Bible or Christian life	10	16
A Christian student group in college	9	53
A Christian student group in high school	6	6

Table 3.10
METHODS OF DISCIPLESHIP WITH SIGNIFICANT IMPACT

Q: Now, among each of the following methods for spiritual growth, which do you think will have a significant impact on developing disciples?

	All Church Leaders	Senior Pastors	Discipleship Leaders
Personal Bible study	92%	91%	96%
Small-group Bible study	88	87	93
Regular one-on-one conversations about discipleship issues with a more mature believer	83	80	90
Teaching the Word in weekly services	81	77	92
One-on-one study with a more mature believer	76	72	87
Memorizing Scripture	65	60	78
Reading Christian books and publications	58	56	63
Listening to media (i.e radio, podcasts, recorded sermons)	45	43	51

4. OBSTACLES

Table 4.1
OBSTACLES TO DISCIPLESHIP: CHURCH LEADERS

Q: There are various things that can get in the way of someone progressing as a disciple. I'm going to read a list of some of these things. For each one, tell me if you think it is a major obstacle, a minor obstacle, or not really an obstacle for people trying to grow as disciples today.
(% major obstacle)

	All Church Leaders	Senior Pastors	Discipleship Leaders
Lack of commitment	87%	86%	88%
Too much busyness in their lives	85	85	84
Sinful habits	70	69	75
Pride that inhibits teachability	70	68	74
Lack of qualified and willing "disciplers"	59	58	64
Lack of supportive relationships	55	53	60
Lack of strong leadership	53	50	61
Negative peer relationships	51	48	60
Lack of a model for discipleship	49	46	55
Fear of vulnerability	47	46	51
Guilt about things in their past	44	42	51
Lack of good resources	18	18	18

Table 4.2
OBSTACLES TO DISCIPLESHIP: CHRISTIAN ADULTS

Q: Now switching gears, I'm going to ask about things that get in the way of your spiritual growth. For each item I read, tell me if this is a major obstacle, a minor obstacle, or not really an obstacle to your spiritual growth.

(% at least somewhat interested in spiritual growth) (major obstacle)

	All Christians	Practicing Christians	Non-practicing Christians
General busyness of life	22%	23%	22%
Spiritual growth will require a lot of hard work	15	16	13
I have had bad past experiences with groups or individuals	12	9	16
Not wanting to think about mistakes you've made in the past	11	10	12
Not wanting to get too personal with other people	11	9	15
My friends are not as interested in spiritual things	10	11	8
I have other more important priorities right now	9	8	10
I can't find a good church or Christian community to join	9	6	16
My family members are not supportive	6	5	8
I would not, or do not, know where to start	6	5	7
I haven't found anyone willing to help me grow spiritually	5	4	6
It's hard to find good resources or information for spiritual growth	5	5	6

Table 4.3
LACK OF MOTIVATION FOR SPIRITUAL GROWTH

Q: For each of the following, please tell me which, if any of these are major reasons that you don't feel compelled to progress in your spiritual life.
(% yes)

	All Christians	Practicing Christians	Non-practicing Christians
I feel comfortable with where I am spiritually	68%	64%	70%
I don't see the benefit of trying to make progress in my spiritual life	16	24	15
One shouldn't have to work at their faith	28	22	29
My previous efforts at making progress in my spiritual life have been unsuccessful	10	22	6
My faith is not such an important part of my life	28	8	32
I have more important things to pay attention to	16	0	21

Table 4.4
REASONS BELIEVERS DO NOT DISCIPLE OTHERS

Q: What gets in the way of mature believers in your church actively discipling younger believers?

	All Church Leaders	Senior Pastors	Discipleship Leaders
Too much busyness in their lives	65%	67%	60%
Lack of commitment	41	44	32
Feelings of inadequacy / unequipped	39	44	24
Fear of vulnerability	18	19	13
Lack of a model for discipleship	17	19	12
Lack of interested "disciples"	17	19	11
Lack of senior leadership endorsement	7	7	8
Lack of good resources	5	6	3
Other	15	13	22
Not sure	2	2	1

Table 4.5
REASONS CHRISTIANS ARE NOT BEING DISCIPLED

Q: Is there any particular reason why you are not being discipled by another person currently?

(% not currently being discipled / mentored)

	All Christians	Practicing Christians	Non-practicing Christians
Just haven't thought about it	29%	29%	29%
Don't think I need it	25	23	29
No one has suggested it	14	15	13
Had a bad experience in the past	2	2	4
Other reason	24	26	20
Not sure	6	6	5

Table 4.6
WHY CHRISTIANS ARE NOT DISCIPLING OTHERS

Q: Is there any particular reason why you are not discipling another person currently?

(% not currently discipling someone else)

	All Christians	Practicing Christians	Non-practicing Christians
Don't think I am qualified / equipped	30%	28%	33%
Just haven't thought about it	23	22	24
No one has suggested it / asked me	20	23	15
Had a bad experience in the past	1	1	2
Other reason	19	20	18
Not sure	7	6	8

5. COMMITMENT

Table 5.1
PRIORITY CHURCH ASSIGNS TO DISCIPLESHIP

	All Church Leaders	Senior Pastors	Discipleship Leaders
Q: What priority does your church place on discipleship, relative to other ministries? Is it . . . ?			
Among the top 3 priorities	61%	62%	58%
The number one priority	26	26	28
Important, not one of the top 3 priorities	8	8	11
Not something you are actively addressing at this time	4	4	4
Not sure	1	1	0

Table 5.2
PERSON PRIMARILY RESPONSIBLE FOR DISCIPLESHIP

	All Church Leaders	Senior Pastors	Discipleship Leaders
Q: Who in your church would you say has primary responsibility for discipleship?			
Senior pastor	49%	55%	33%
Sunday school / life groups	20	19	21
Eldership / deacons	11	10	15
Discipleship pastor	8	4	20
Other	10	9	12
Not sure	2	2	1

Table 5.3
DESIRED CHANGES IN HOW THE CHURCH DISCIPLES

Q: If your church could do one thing differently when it comes to how it disciples, what would you want to change?

	All Church Leaders	Senior Pastors	Discipleship Leaders
Develop a more clearly articulated plan, or approach to discipleship	27%	28%	23%
More interest in becoming a disciple	16	17	11
More well-trained lay leaders	10	11	8
More volunteers	7	7	8
Senior leadership modeling discipleship better	5	4	8
More programs	3	3	5
Undertake regular assessments of progress	2	2	2
Senior leadership endorsement	1	2	1
More paid staff	1	1	2
More money to spend on purchasing resources	1	1	1
Other	22	20	29
Not sure	4	4	2

7. RESOURCES

Table 7.1
PERCENT OF BUDGET SPENT ON DISCIPLESHIP

	All Church Leaders	Senior Pastors	Discipleship Leaders
Q: About what percent of your church's operational budget is spent on programs or resources specifically aimed at discipleship?			
Less than 10 percent	27%	26%	29%
10 to 19 percent	29	30	27
20 to 29 percent	18	20	15
30 percent or more	26	24	28
Mean	21	21	22
Median	15	15	15

Table 7.2
VALUE OF A SYSTEMATIC CURRICULUM OR PROGRAM OF DISCIPLESHIP

	All Church Leaders	Senior Pastors	Discipleship Leaders
Q: In your experience, how valuable is it for someone to be involved in a systematic curriculum or program for discipleship?			
Very valuable	59%	59%	60%
Somewhat valuable	34	33	35
Not too valuable	5	6	3
Not at all valuable	1	1	2
Not sure	1	2	0

Table 7.3
OPINION ON THE AMOUNT OF DISCIPLESHIP PROGRAMS

	All Church Leaders	Senior Pastors	Discipleship Leaders
Q: Overall, do you think there are too many discipleship resources and programs out there, not enough resources and programs, or about the right amount?			
About right	46%	44%	52%
Not enough	21	22	19
Too many	19	18	22
Not sure	14	17	7

Table 7.4
FAMILIARITY WITH DISCIPLESHIP ORGANIZATIONS

Q: How familiar are you with the following organizations? (church leaders)**
Q: Are you familiar with . . . ? (adults)

	All Church Leaders	Senior Pastors	Discipleship Leaders	All Christians	Practicing Christians	Non-practicing Christians
Promise Keepers	92%	93%	91%	39%	43%	34%
Fellowship of Christian Athletes	84	85	83	38	41	31
Cru (formerly Campus Crusade)	81	80	81	24	31	13
InterVarsity	72	73	69	12	14	10
Navigators	72	73	67	15	17	11
Bible Study Fellowship	47	46	50	31	32	29
Alpha	41	41	41	9	10	9
Ligonier Ministries	34	34	36	8	9	6
Renovare	19	20	16	2	2	2
Scripture Union	13	13	12	6	6	6

** Church leader study includes those very or somewhat familiar.

Table 7.5
FAMILIARITY WITH DISCIPLESHIP ORGANIZATIONS:
CHURCH LEADERS

Q: How familiar are you with the following organizations?

	All Church Leaders	Senior Pastors	Discipleship Leaders
Promise Keepers			
very familiar	39%	39%	38%
somewhat familiar	53	53	53
not familiar / not sure	8	7	9
Fellowship of Christian Athletes			
very familiar	35	34	38
somewhat familiar	49	51	45
not familiar / not sure	16	15	18
Cru (formerly Campus Crusade)			
very familiar	27	26	31
somewhat familiar	54	55	51
not familiar / not sure	19	20	19
Navigators			
very familiar	24	23	25
somewhat familiar	48	50	42
not familiar / not sure	29	27	33
InterVarsity			
very familiar	22	21	25
somewhat familiar	50	52	44
not familiar	28	27	31

Table 7.5
FAMILIARITY WITH DISCIPLESHIP ORGANIZATIONS:
CHURCH LEADERS (CONTINUED)

	All Church Leaders	Senior Pastors	Discipleship Leaders
Bible Study Fellowship			
very familiar	15	14	17
somewhat familiar	33	32	33
not familiar / not sure	53	54	50
Alpha			
very familiar	13%	12%	14%
somewhat familiar	29	29	28
not familiar / not sure	59	59	59
Ligonier Ministries			
very familiar	9	9	10
somewhat familiar	25	25	26
not familiar / not sure	66	66	64
Renovare			
very familiar	6	6	6
somewhat familiar	13	14	10
not familiar / not sure	81	80	84
Scripture Union			
very familiar	3	3	2
somewhat familiar	10	10	10
not familiar / not sure	87	87	88

Table 7.6
IMPRESSIONS OF DISCIPLESHIP ORGANIZATIONS

Q: What is your impression of this organization?
% very positive (among those familiar with organization)

	All Church Leaders	Senior Pastors	Discipleship Leaders	All Christians
Renovare	39%	38%	NA	NA
Fellowship of Christian Athletes	35	35	31	46
Navigators	35	33	42	35
Bible Study Fellowship	33	31	42	53
Cru (formerly Campus Crusade)	31	30	35	37
Ligonier Ministries	32	29	NA	34
Alpha	29	28	NA	25
InterVarsity	28	27	32	35
Promise Keepers	24	23	27	39
Scripture Union	17	19	NA	43

NA: not shown due to limited sample size.

Table 7.7
BEST DISCIPLESHIP ORGANIZATIONS

Q: Which one or two organizations would you say are best at enabling discipleship?
(among those familiar with at least two organizations)

	All Church Leaders	Senior Pastors	Discipleship Leaders	All Christians	Practicing Christians	Non-practicing Christians
Navigators	26%	26%	27%	8%	10%	5%
Cru (formerly Campus Crusade)	20	19	23	15	17	8
Fellowship of Christian Athletes	17	17	18	22	22	23
Promise Keepers	15	16	14	25	28	18
InterVarsity	14	13	18	5	6	2
Alpha	12	11	15	3	3	4
Bible Study Fellowship	11	11	13	31	28	39
Renovare	6	6	5	1	1	1
Ligonier Ministries	5	5	6	3	3	3
Scripture Union	1	2	0	2	2	4
Other	5	6	3	NA	NA	NA
None of these	9	9	9	10	8	14
Not sure	12	14	5	4	4	5

NA: Option not presented in adult survey.

Table 7.8
USE OF NAVIGATORS PROGRAMS

Q: Has your church ever used any of the following discipleship resources? *(church leaders)*

Q: Have you ever used any of the following discipleship resources? *(adults whose spiritual growth is at least somewhat important)*

	All Church Leaders	Senior Pastors	Discipleship Leaders	All Christians	Practicing Christians	Non-practicing Christians
Life Change Series	11%	12%	9%	6%	7%	3%
Design for Discipleship	9	9	10	4	5	2
Studies in Christian Living	10	8	15	9	11	6
Topical Memory System	6	7	5	4	5	2
The 2:7 Series	7	6	9	3	3	2
Ways of the Alongsider	1	1	0	1	1	1
None of these	73	73	71	83	81	88

Table 7.9
HELPFULNESS OF NAVIGATORS PROGRAMS

Q: How helpful was [program]?
(% "very helpful" among those who had used each program)

	All Church Leaders	All Christians
Topical Memory System	35%	56%
The 2:7 Series	31	NA
Life Change Series	31	46
Design for Discipleship	29	55
Studies in Christian Living	20	50
Ways of the Alongsider	NA	NA

NA: not shown due to limited sample size.

DEMOGRAPHICS

DEMOGRAPHIC PROFILE OF CHURCH LEADERS

	All Church Leaders	Senior Pastors	Discipleship Leaders
Age			
Under 40	16%	12%	30%
40 to 59	51	53	46
60 and older	33	36	24
Median age (in years)	54	56	49
Gender			
Male	91	93	85
Female	10	8	15
Employment			
Full-time, paid	85	87	80
Other	15	13	20
Denominational Segment			
Mainline	22	26	11
Non-Mainline	78	74	89
Attendance			
Less than 100	40	47	22
100 to 499	50	50	49
500 plus	10	3	29

DEMOGRAPHIC PROFILE OF CHURCH LEADERS
(CONTINUED)

	All Church Leaders	Senior Pastors	Discipleship Leaders
Church operating budget			
Less than $100K	17	19	11
$100K to $499K	54	60	36
$500K plus	29	21	53
Region			
Northeast	13	14	9
Midwest	28	25	36
South	47	48	43
West	13	13	12
Pastor's ethnicity			
White	84%	85%	82%
Black	10	10	9
Hispanic	2	2	2
Congregation's ethnicity			
White	82	82	80
Black	9	9	9
Hispanic	2	1	2

DEMOGRAPHIC PROFILE OF U.S. CHRISTIANS

	All Christians	Practicing Christians	Non-practicing Christians
Age			
Millennial (18-30)	17%	14%	21%
Gen-Xer (31-49)	28	29	27
Boomer (50-68)	39	39	39
Elder (69 plus)	16	19	12
Median age (in years)	51	52	50
Marital status			
Married	56	61	49
All Single	44	39	51
Never married	23	20	27
Ever divorced	24	23	26
Children under 18 in household			
Yes	28	28	26
No	72	72	74

DEMOGRAPHIC PROFILE OF U.S. CHRISTIANS (CONTINUED)

	All Christians	Practicing Christians	Non-practicing Christians
Region			
Northeast	20	20	21
Midwest	25	26	24
South	36	38	32
West	19	16	23
Ethnicity			
White	68	68	68
Black	13	16	8
Hispanic	16	13	19
All Non-white	32	32	31

THEOLOGRAPHIC PROFILE OF U.S. CHRISTIANS

	All Christians	Practicing Christians	Non-practicing Christians
Denominational segment			
Protestant	72%	75%	66%
Catholic	28	25	34
Protestant, Mainline	19	20	18
Protestant, Non-Mainline	41	48	30
Median age (in years)	51	52	50
Belief segment			
Evangelical	12	18	2
Non-evangelical born again	44	50	32
Notional Christian	45	32	66

B. EDUCATORS

DEFINING DISCIPLESHIP

Educators' definitions of discipleship are wide-ranging and even conflicting, especially with regard to the optimal number and types of participants. Most emphasize the "heart" of discipleship (growing deeper in relationship with Christ), while some refer to outward manifestations of growth (obedience to God's Word, serving others, living a life "worth imitating"). Many focus on "becoming a disciple" or "becoming a follower of Jesus," which requires growing in Christ-likeness through study (individual or with others), community and obedience. Two educators cite the importance of both "vertical" (with God) and "horizontal" (with believers) discipleship.

The widest disagreement on definitions centers on whether discipleship requires individual attention and encouragement (one-on-one or "life-on-life"), or if it can happen between peers or in small, or even larger, groups. According to various educators we interviewed, discipleship may consist primarily of new-believer education or entail spiritual development or "formation" anywhere in one's faith journey.

Some, but not all, draw distinctions between discipleship (training up a younger/less mature believer) and disciple-*making* (focused on conversion). Others prefer a broader, generational approach to discipleship, where faith is passed down from mature believers. A small proportion draws no distinction between the terms. "Spiritual parenting," based on 1 Thessalonians 2:3-13, is mentioned by a few.

All agree that Jesus commanded his followers to make disciples; therefore, discipleship is not *optional*.

BARRIERS

Most educators lament churches that approach discipleship from a programmatic standpoint, believing that, in general, programs are too "cookie-cutter" and can even hinder real discipleship by taking up precious time. Accountability, vulnerability and intentionality are considered by many to be essential—and these are difficult to achieve through structured programs. Further, discipleship is ongoing—a process that should continue throughout the course of life—whereas programs can lend themselves to a "tick the box" mentality.

- Thus, educators most commonly cite "church programs" when asked to identify the most significant barriers to effective discipleship. Other barriers include:
- Overly formalized processes (rather than organic approaches that enable deeper, more meaningful, Spirit-led relationships)
- Hyper-focus on evangelism and conversion, to the detriment of ongoing nurture
- Overemphasis on worship and experiential spirituality; consumerist approach to church
- Church leaders not modeling and/or championing discipleship
- Potential disciplers feeling under-equipped, not qualified or spiritually unready
- Impatience, especially on the part of younger Christians
- General "busyness" of life and an unwillingness to invest the considerable amount of time required for real spiritual growth
- Distractions from media that prevent believers from learning how to really read and "dig into" the Bible (despite access through media to useful biblical tools)
- Individualistic nature of society, especially among Millennials (however, some point to a greater desire among young adults for meaningful relationships—a desire which the church can fulfill especially well through discipleship)

MODELS

As for the optimal format for discipleship, educators' preferences vary, and most believe flexibility is important. Quite a few have expanded their definition of discipleship from a one-on-one "Paul-Timothy" style to more communal and peer-to-peer. Educators are nearly evenly split on the *single most* impactful approach to discipleship: 1) one-on-one Bible study with a more mature believer, 2) regular one-on-one conversations about discipleship issues with a more mature believer or 3) small group Bible study.

Most say two or more of these, as well as personal Bible study and memorizing Scripture, can be very effective. Several mention the notion of "iron sharpening iron" through peer relationships, while others insist the passing of faith from older to younger believers remains an essential tenet of discipleship. Whichever model is preferred, the majority of educators consider community essential to spiritual growth. Biblical support includes Ecclesiastes 4:9-12, Ephesians 4, 2 Timothy 2:2 and Jesus' model of discipling 12 men recounted in the Gospels.

RESOURCES

Among educators the most appreciated, frequently cited writers and books about discipleship are:

- Dallas Willard, *The Spirit of the Disciplines*
- Richard Foster, *Celebration of Discipline*
- Greg Ogden, *Transforming Discipleship*

The majority of educators also refer to their own personal growth in defining discipleship. Many say where they once considered biblical education, transmission of knowledge, worship or general church programming as essential means of discipleship, they now better appreciate the slow, transforming work of the Spirit. Further, they say that slow work happens more often through life experiences and relationships rather than through programming. A few are excited about the opportunities to reinvigorate the practice of discipleship based on this deeper, more God-dependent definition.

Most express concerns about the state of discipleship in the U.S. The following sentiments are emblematic of a widespread outlook: "The church in America will die, and the Church in other countries will flourish.... I see widespread neglect excused by busy-ness, an emphasis on worship or preaching or multi-site churches where pastors don't know parishioners or farm out ministry to others."

Educators demonstrate a diversity of opinions about what discipleship is and how it should be carried out. Additionally, the number and nature of barriers that concern educators suggest a fresh look at discipleship is much needed.

C.
EXEMPLARS

Overall, exemplars exhibit more continuity of response than educators. While not all of their approaches to discipleship are the same, they share in common a clear vision and commitment, which permeates the culture of exemplary organizations.

VISION

For exemplar churches and organizations, discipleship is not a program or even a "ministry"; it is the foundation upon which the church rests. There is vision among the senior leadership for what healthy discipleship should look like, and this appears to trickle down to the entire body.

In general, the tone and nature of responses indicate that discipleship is a topic leaders have thought about at length, have a perspective on and maintain a passion for. They believe making and growing disciples is Jesus' singular commission to the Church, and they are *intentional* about it. Three-quarters of exemplar churches say senior leadership vision or endorsement and a clearly articulated plan or approach to discipleship are critical to their efforts.

COMMITMENT

Additionally, the church's priority on overall spiritual development reflects a clear commitment to discipleship—not just at the leadership level, but throughout the congregation. Two-thirds of exemplar churches say discipleship is among the top three priorities for their senior pastor; one-third considers it *the* top priority.

Three-quarters or more of exemplar churches say the following are critical to their discipleship efforts:

- Senior leaders who model discipleship
- Church-wide commitment to the Scriptures
- Well-trained lay leaders

On average, more than half of exemplar church members are involved in some sort of discipleship group or relationship. It is estimated that congregants spend an average of two to three hours per week (outside of church) devoted to spiritual development.

DEFINING DISCIPLESHIP

Exemplars' definitions of discipleship share a similar vision and approach, but they are not prescriptive as to the *nature* of discipleship groups or relationships. Many respondents say flexible design is important to meet the changing needs of individuals or communities. Some key themes and descriptors mentioned include:

- Following Jesus; becoming more like him
- Growing, maturing, pursuing and exhibiting life change *for the purpose* of showing others who Jesus is
- Relational, "caught, not taught"
- Generational, passed down from one believer to the next

Most exemplar leaders say their definition has changed over time. Many have shifted away from an emphasis on "head knowledge" toward life transformation, usually in the context of relationship. Some say their definition has expanded from individual growth in Christ to include "making disciples." This is because real, healthy disciples should naturally produce more disciples. More than half refer to "making disciples" as an important component of discipleship.

MODELS

The composition and nature of discipleship groups or relationships varies. A portion of exemplars prefers the mature-to-new believer relationship, usually one-on-one. More use *both* this approach and the peer-to-peer/small group model, which is believed to be more appealing to members. However, only two among 37 respondents use the peer/small group format alone. Exemplars widely consider a one-on-one component—whether Bible study or conversation—essential to fruitful discipleship.

Exemplar leaders also feel strongly about the role of community, or the church body, in discipleship. Some describe the church as an "equipping station" from which members are launched into the "world" (workplace, neighborhood, school, etc.) as an "ambassador of Christ." Many talk about the importance of the body in encouraging each other to be on mission and to grow in their spiritual lives.

In order to ensure healthy growth, exemplars invest significantly in leadership development (aka "disciple-making"). Many say this expectation is set when individuals join a group or initiate a discipleship relationship. Participants are ultimately expected to go on to disciple others. This is a key measure of success for most exemplars. Many also have leadership classes or other training regimens specifically for discipleship leaders.

ASSESSMENT

Exemplars tend to be quite intentional about tracking the progress of discipleship in their churches. This is accomplished in part by observing "soft" measures: fruits of the Spirit lived out among members, passion for sharing faith, individuals making God-honoring life decisions. Participation and leadership are the most common objective indicators: the number engaged in small groups or Bible studies, the number of new leaders and the number of individuals serving inside and outside the church. Additionally, approximately half of churches use surveys or self-assessments.

Leaders of exemplar churches offer a vision of what good discipleship looks like and demonstrate that a variety of models can prove fruitful. It is clear from their responses that there are no shortcuts to producing disciples of Christ; hard work is non-negotiable. Exemplar churches and organizations are committed to this work and so create a culture of disciple-making.

D.
METHODOLOGIES

The data contained in this report originated through a series of research studies conducted by Barna Group. The study was commissioned by NavPress for The Navigators.

The full project was completed in multiple stages. To begin, 36 educators from Protestant and Catholic seminaries and Bible colleges completed an online survey of open-ended questions during December 2014 and January 2015. These findings were used to revise and conduct an open-ended survey with exemplar churches and ministries.

Leaders of 30 churches and seven parachurch ministries that exemplify excellence in discipleship completed an open-ended, online survey February 3 to March 4, 2015. Respondents were recruited from a list developed by Navigators' staff as well as nominated by Protestant pastors from Barna's Pastor Panel.

Following these two qualitative studies, an online and telephone survey was conducted among 615 Protestant senior pastors and 218 discipleship pastors. Churches were contacted from a random list of U.S. Protestant churches, with approximately 543 interviews conducted by phone and 290 online. The interviews were conducted between April 7 and May 30, 2015.

At the same time, a nationwide study of Christian adults ages 18 and older was conducted using an online panel and phone interviews (with a mix of 60% landline and 40% cell phone). Surveys for this portion of the research study were completed between March 26 and April 15, 2015. A total of 2,013 surveys were completed: 1,300 online and 703 via phone. The sample error on this survey is plus or minus 3.1 percent points at the 95-percent confidence level. Data were weighted by age, gender, etc., to be representative of all U.S. Christians ages 18 and older.

Survey calls were made at various times during the day (for churches) and evenings (for adults), so that every individual selected for inclusion was contacted up to five separate days, at different times of the day, to maximize the possibility of contact. This is a quality control procedure to ensure that individuals in the sampling frame have an equivalent probability of inclusion within the survey, thereby increasing the survey reliability. All of the interviews were conducted by experienced, trained interviewers who were supervised at all times; every interviewer was monitored during their performance on the project. The survey was conducted through the use of a CATI (Computer Assisted Telephone Interviewing) system. This system ensures that question skip patterns are properly administered by interviewers and that survey data are recorded accurately.

The online portion of the study was conducted among a representative random sample of adults and churches using a web-enabled consumer panel.

ABOUT **BARNA**

Barna Group is a research firm dedicated to providing actionable insights on faith and culture with a particular focus on the Christian church. In its 30-year history, Barna Group has conducted more than one million interviews in the course of hundreds of studies, and has become a go-to source for organizations that want to better understand a complex and changing world.

Our clients include a broad range of academic institutions, churches, non-profits, and businesses, such as Alpha, the Templeton Foundation, Pepperdine University, Fuller Seminary, the Bill and Melinda Gates Foundation, the Maclellan Foundation, DreamWorks Animation, Focus Features, Habitat for Humanity, NBC-Universal, the ONE Campaign, Paramount Pictures, the Salvation Army, Walden Media, Sony and World Vision.

The firm's studies are frequently quoted by major media outlets such as *The Economist*, BBC, CNN, *USA Today, the Wall Street Journal*, Fox News, Huffington Post, *The New York Times* and the *Los Angeles Times*.

Barna Group's work reaches around the world through the efforts of **Barna Global**. Current Barna Global projects include engagements in Scotland, England, Australia and South Africa.

Learn more about Barna Group at www.barna.org.